MASTERING MICROSOFT FLIGHT SIMULATOR 2024 FOR BEGINNERS

Step By Step Guide to Experience Unmatched Realism, Stunning Landscapes, And Advanced Flight Technology

Copyright © 2024 **Marc Vellander**

All Rights Reserved

This book or parts thereof may not be reproduced in any form, stored in any retrieval system, or transmitted in any form by any means—electronic, mechanical, photocopy, recording, or otherwise—without prior written permission of the publisher, except as provided by United States of America copyright law and fair use.

Disclaimer and Terms of Use

The author and publisher of this book and the accompanying materials have used their best efforts in preparing this book. The author and publisher make no representation or warranties with respect to the accuracy, applicability, fitness, or completeness of the contents of this book. The information contained in this book is strictly for informational purposes. Therefore, if you wish to apply the ideas contained in this book, you are taking full responsibility for your actions.

Printed in the United States of America

TABLE OF CONTENT

TABLE OF CONTENT III

MICROSOFT FLIGHT SIMULATOR 2024 OVERVIEW 1

   WELCOME TO MICROSOFT FLIGHT SIMULATOR 2024 2
   OVERVIEW OF THE GUIDE AND HOW TO USE IT 4
   HIGHLIGHTS OF THE NEW FEATURES IN MSFS 2024 8

CHAPTER 1 11

GETTING STARTED WITH MSFS 2024 11

   WHAT YOU NEED FOR A FLIGHT SIMULATOR 12
      What's the Cost of a Home Flight Simulator? 14
      PC, Mac, or Xbox: Which Should You Choose? 18
      What's the Best Flight Simulator for You? 18
      DCS World 21
   ADVANCED AVIONICS SETUPS 24
   SYSTEM REQUIREMENTS AND INSTALLATION 26
   MINIMUM SYSTEM REQUIREMENTS 27
   EXPLORING THE GAME INTERFACE 29
   RECOMMENDED SYSTEM REQUIREMENTS 29

CHAPTER 2 33

BASICS OF FLIGHT SIMULATION 33

      Understanding Aerodynamics in the Virtual World 36
   AIRCRAFT CATEGORIES: FROM PROPS TO JETS 40
   ALL MEANINGS OF "AIRCRAFT CATEGORY" 44
   THE ROLE OF WEATHER AND NAVIGATION 46

CHAPTER 3 49

SETTING UP FOR REALISM 49

   FINAL DESTINATIONS 51
   GRAPHICS AND PERFORMANCE OPTIMIZATION 52
      Customizing Controls and Hotkeys 56
   ADD-ONS AND MODS FOR ENHANCED GAMEPLAY 59

CHAPTER 4 66

AIRCRAFT DEEP DIVE **66**

    GENERAL AVIATION AIRCRAFT OVERVIEW 67

    COMMERCIAL AIRLINERS: COCKPITS AND FEATURES 68

        In a Nutshell: Knowing the Cockpit 71

        Determining the Role of the Yoke in Aircraft Control 72

        Unique Components of a Propeller Plane Cockpit 74

CHAPTER 5 .... **77**

NAVIGATING THE WORLD **77**

    REAL-WORLD MAPS AND FLIGHT PATHS 79

    USING THE WORLD MAP INTERFACE 84

CHAPTER 6 .... **91**

ADVANCED PILOTING TECHNIQUES **91**

Understanding Crosswind Operations 94

    IFR VS. VFR FLYING 97

    STAYING SAFE WITH VFR FLYING 100

    EMERGENCY PROCEDURES AND FAILURES 103

CHAPTER 7 .... **109**

EXPLORING GLOBAL DESTINATIONS **109**

    FAMOUS AIRPORTS AND CITIES 111

    HIDDEN GEMS, LESSER-KNOWN LOCATIONS 115

CHAPTER 8 .... **118**

MULTIPLAYER AND COMMUNITY FEATURES **118**

    JOINING THE MSFS COMMUNITY 119

    REAL-TIME MULTIPLAYER FLIGHTS 122

CHAPTER 9 .... **126**

TRAINING AND LEARNING MODULES **126**

        Built-In Flight Lessons and Tutorials [Free] 129

    TYPES OF FLIGHT SIMULATORS 134

    ENHANCING SKILLS WITH AI ASSISTANCE 136

    CERTIFICATION CHALLENGES AND ACHIEVEMENTS 139

CHAPTER 10 141

USING VIRTUAL REALITY AND IMMERSIVE TOOLS 141

Setting Up VR for MSFS 2024 143
MSFS2024 In-Game Settings for Most GPUs 151
Minimum PC Requirements for MSFS2024 in VR 152
Why MSFS 2024 Is a Great VR Choice 153
Immersive Cockpit Experiences 154
Enhancing Gameplay with Third-Party Tools 155

CHAPTER 11 158

CUSTOMIZATION AND MODDING 158

Using SDK for Advanced Modding 160

INDEX 168

MICROSOFT FLIGHT SIMULATOR 2024 OVERVIEW

Buckle up to take the ultimate journey with virtual aviation. Microsoft Flight Simulator 2024 isn't just a game; instead, it's an experience that puts you in the captain's seat of nearly any aircraft while giving you the freedom of exploring the world from up above.

Whether you're tracing actual flight paths or simply taking off to see your hometown from a bird's-eye view, the possibilities are endless—as long as you've got the fuel to keep going!

Each aircraft is carefully crafted to mimic the performance and handling of its real-world counterpart, making this simulator so realistic that even budding pilots use it as a training tool.

It goes beyond just flying anywhere with the introduction of aviation careers. Now, you will be able to put your skills to the test in roles such as Search and Rescue, Cargo Transport, or even an Air Ambulance pilot. These new features add more meaning and realism to your flights, offering challenges that go far beyond casual exploration.

Looking for the latest MSFS2024 helicopter mods and news all in one place? You're in the right spot! We've got a wide selection of mods designed to enhance your experience, each with unique features and specifications to suit your needs. Finding the perfect add-on to elevate your game is simple—just browse, pick your favorite, and hit the download button. Follow the easy steps, and you're ready to take off.

WELCOME TO MICROSOFT FLIGHT SIMULATOR 2024

Microsoft Flight Simulator 2024, launching on Tuesday, November 19, 2024, is packed with exciting features that promise to redefine virtual aviation. From its groundbreaking "digital twin" representation of Earth to stunning graphical enhancements, including ultra-detailed ground textures, realistic vertical obstructions, and the addition of diverse animal species, there's so much to look forward to. But the cherry on the cake for most, including myself, has to be the highly awaited Career Mode: a feature that finally enables you to live a life as a virtual aviator from your couch. While Career Mode isn't entirely new to the franchise—earlier versions, such as FSX released in 2006, also included missions and rewards—its return is significant. According to Jorg Neumann, head of Microsoft Flight Simulator, "The idea for Missions, or an Aviation Career," he says, "was indeed spawned during our work on MSFS 2020, but decided to focus on the core innovations of creating Earth's digital twin from satellite imagery with digital elevation maps powered by Bing.

We knew we had to focus on perfecting the foundation first," explains Neumann. "Once MSFS 2020 launched successfully and we had established a steady rhythm of updates, we revisited the idea of missions and careers, ready to take it to the next level."

Now, Career Mode is set to give players an immersive and rewarding experience, building well from where its predecessor set the foundation.

Microsoft Flight Simulator 2024 is built on a foundation of authenticity, from the realistic physics and atmospheric systems to the avionics and overall experience. As the team started designing Career Mode, it was approached with the same dedication to realism that shaped MSFS 2020.

We saw an opportunity to do something groundbreaking, which no one has done before in terms of missions and activities with regard to entertainment software," said Jorg Neumann, Head of Microsoft Flight Simulator. "By building a digital replica of the entire planet, we could let players start their career anywhere on Earth and integrate dynamic elements like seasons, weather, time of day, and specific locations into the missions.

Extensive surveys were conducted within the community to make sure they were delivering what players really wanted. From hardcore simmers to casual gamers and digital tourists, the message was loud and clear: players wanted goals. They wanted purpose in their flights. This overwhelming response sealed the deal on making Career Mode a key feature in MSFS 2024, offering players structured objectives while preserving the authentic simulation experience, they value.

The passion of the aviation community has been invaluable to the development of both Career Mode and the overall flight simulation experience," said Jorg Neumann, Head of Microsoft Flight Simulator. "We have been fortunate to gain amazing insights from pilots in all areas of rotorcraft, agricultural aviation, firefighting, skydiving, and commercial airlines. Simmers have also provided valuable insight through user research and community forums into what they need, issues they face, and what suggestions they have. The active participation of the aviation world keeps us motivated and helps drive innovation in the simulator.

Well, it is designed that Career Mode in Microsoft Flight Simulator 2024 is for everyone, whatever one's experience. It means beginners can just plunge into the fray without any prerequisites, beginning as a rookie and progressively improving through training. In fact, these training sessions, of which about 54 courses are available, help one build confidence and prepare to take the certification exams to be allowed into advanced activities.

Experienced simmers or real-world pilots can immediately jump into certification exams and take on more challenging roles, such as piloting commercial airliners. To make things even more balanced, missions have difficulty ratings to prevent less experienced players from encountering scenarios they may not yet be equipped to handle, such as poor weather conditions.

OVERVIEW OF THE GUIDE AND HOW TO USE IT

The passion of the aviation community has been invaluable to the development of both Career Mode and the overall flight simulation experience," said Jorg Neumann, Head of Microsoft Flight Simulator. "We have been fortunate to gain amazing insights from pilots in all areas of rotorcraft, agricultural aviation, firefighting, skydiving, and commercial airlines. Simmers have also provided valuable insight through user research and community forums into what they need, issues they face, and what suggestions they have. The active participation of the aviation world keeps us motivated and helps drive innovation in the simulator.

Well, it is designed that Career Mode in Microsoft Flight Simulator 2024 is for everyone, whatever one's experience. It means beginners can just plunge into the fray without any prerequisites, beginning as a rookie and progressively improving through training. In fact, these training sessions, of which about 54 courses are available, help one build confidence and prepare to take the certification exams to be allowed into advanced activities.

Experienced simmers or real-world pilots can immediately jump into certification exams and take on more challenging roles, such as piloting commercial airliners. To make things even more balanced, missions have difficulty ratings to prevent less experienced players from encountering scenarios they may not yet be equipped to handle, such as poor weather conditions.

Microsoft Flight Simulator 2024 takes the art of realism to higher echelons in reality-affecting scenarios; for instance, crop-dusting missions based on real-world detection of fields with complex machine learning will also be available, while every airliner mission available in Career Mode mirrors what has happened or is occurring within real life. For accuracy, the team consulted experts across many fields to authentically capture the stakes and nuances of these roles and translate them into the simulator.

Turning this vision into reality has been a massive undertaking for the development team. A major breakthrough came when a search-and-rescue (SAR) pilot tested an early version of the simulator.

He came back and told us it was an incredible experience and very close to reality, to real-world SAR flying," says Jorg Neumann. "It was quite an exciting moment for the team to understand that we were on par.

Other milestones included the visit to the Sécurité Civile operations center in France, where firefighting pilots tested the missions and, although they did comment on aspects for improvement, their overall reactions were extremely positive.

"These validation moments were essential," Neumann adds. "Our goal isn't just to create engaging missions for players—it's to replicate, as closely as possible, the real-world experiences of pilots. That's the level of authenticity we're striving for."

The wait for Microsoft Flight Simulator 2024 is finally coming to a close, and Jorg Neumann himself points out the thrill of finally seeing players dive into their own virtual aviation careers when it launches on November 19, 2024.

"This is what it's all about," Neumann explains. "Using advanced technology, the digital twin of Earth, and the data at our disposal, we've crafted an experience that delivers on the franchise's commitment to realism. It's something truly unique, and as creators, seeing it come to life is the ultimate reward."

Pre-orders for Microsoft Flight Simulator 2024 are live now in the Microsoft Store, and the game will be launching across several different editions. The Standard Edition includes 70 aircraft and 150 upgraded airports and will be available on day one with Game Pass. Pre-orders also include the De Havilland Canada CL-415 firefighting aircraft, ready to use in Microsoft Flight Simulator (2020).

Other editions include:

Deluxe Edition: Adds 10 more aircraft and 5 extra airports.

Premium Deluxe Edition: Adds 15 more aircraft for a total of 95.

Aviator Edition: Includes everything from the Premium Deluxe Edition, plus 30 Marketplace aircraft that came out between 2021-2024.

For owners of the Deluxe and Premium Deluxe Editions of Microsoft Flight Simulator (2020), all the aircraft and airports exclusive to their packages will automatically transfer into Microsoft Flight Simulator 2024, making it easy for them to continue flying like they did before.

Wloch presented the need for cloud-based downloads of data within Microsoft Flight Simulator 2024 as a consequence of the size of the title, making reliance on the purely streaming world data solution utilized in MSFS 2020 unrealistic. If the complete Standard Edition of MSFS 2024 had to be downloaded in a manner similar to that used in MSFS 2020-installed sans cloud-provided world data-the download would involve 1.4 Terabytes and take no less than 25 hours at the server speed of today.

To decrease download times, Wloch suggested increasing the size of the rolling cache to something like 128 GB. In addition, players will be able to manually install selected packages, such as aircraft and airports, as in MSFS 2020, but this will be optional. Players will also be able to completely deactivate any package, which will not be installed or streamed, and this functionality is expected to arrive in a mid-December patch. Streaming packages will, of course, be available as usual for those who want it.

The current rolling cache is about 80% efficient, though there are issues with MIP streaming of textures, which the team is working to optimize. There are also some LOD issues, particularly due to CDN server limitations in the initial days after launch, which should improve over time.

Another concern is low framerates with Dynamic Settings. In case of low framerates being detected, the system reduces details by switching over to lower LOD assets; this may improve if the feature is disabled.

On Xbox, it's prone to running out of memory after long play sessions with the quick resume feature, which doesn't clean up memory. While restarting the game manually might solve this, the developers are looking for a solution that handles this automatically.

Asobo also focuses on memory optimization, which is currently a top priority in the team. Official Marketplace opens its gates in early 2025, which allows the developers to spend more time testing their add-ons.

The third patch will include a partial fix for overly bright airport and night lighting. A more permanent solution to this problem, possibly involving the creation of new ground textures for night scenes worldwide, is still under investigation.

HIGHLIGHTS OF THE NEW FEATURES IN MSFS 2024

With the release of Microsoft Flight Simulator 2024 imminent, it is fair to say that excitement in the community is building and we're no different here at FSElite. So, with a number of hours to go, here's what we're most looking forward to trying out in MSFS 2024:

1. Thin Client Technology

One of the biggest upgrades in MSFS 2024 is the move toward "Thin Client" technology. MSFS 2020 required a whopping 150 GB download, but MSFS 2024 will only require 50 GB of storage upon launch. In essence, the game will be able to stream more from the cloud rather than requiring such large files stored on your PC. Of course, be prepared with a good connection.

2. A Wide Range of New Aircraft

MSFS 2024 will provide an impressive range of aircraft starting with 70 for the Standard Edition. Players using Digital Deluxe, Premium Deluxe, or Aviator Editions will be able to use even more aircraft. Newcomers include the Airbus A330, Boeing 737 MAX 8, PC-12 NGX, and Cirrus VisionJet, while other classic favorites such as the TBM-930 and DA-62 have been brought up to modern standards. Thanks to partnerships with third-party developers like iniBuilds and Carenado, MSFS 2024 promises even higher-quality aircraft.

3. A Stunning New World

Visual upgrades are taken to the next level in MSFS 2024. The world itself isn't different, but the graphics sure have. For one, ground textures are made up of 3D polygons now and feature bumpiness, cracks, tire marks, and all sorts of stuff. It includes new satellite imagery, far more accurate cities, and AI-powered technologies, among many others. Expect new biomes, fresh vegetation, and improved weather effects including realistic lighting, cirrus clouds, and ray tracing for sharper shadows.

4. Enhanced Flight Dynamics

Flight dynamics are a very critical aspect of any flight simulator, and MSFS 2024 does it so much better than its predecessor. Introducing new physics methods such as rigid and soft body simulations, updates to CFD, aircraft behavior is much more realistic. You'll experience how terrain, weather, and turbulence affect your plane's performance, and even how cargo or G-forces can impact flight. In addition to these physics upgrades, aircraft systems like electrical, fuel, and hydraulic systems have been overhauled, and the simulator now includes a new payload and wear-and-tear system. The new electronic flight bag and flight planning tool will also make flight planning and in-flight management more realistic and user-friendly. Microsoft Flight Simulator 2024 is shaping up to be a truly groundbreaking release, and we can't wait to dive into all the new features it has to offer.

5. Activities and Career Mode

Not sure where to begin in Microsoft Flight Simulator 2024? The game introduces new activities and an exciting career mode to get you started. In Career Mode, you can choose an airport to begin your virtual pilot journey. From there, you'll complete missions and tasks to earn certifications. Of course, with progress and experience earned you may achieve game money, which should be spent to buy new aircraft and unlock missions. You will have several different types of missions: to carry advertisement banners, extinguish fires, perform rescuing tasks, and the like. If you don't want to, you are welcome to follow the airliner route, working your way from air Cadet up. The skill tree gives you the freedom to specialize in the direction you want, while missions are dynamically generated, taking into consideration live weather and seasonal conditions at locations around the world.

If you are not into career mode, then you can freely roam the world as you want. Free flight mode remains there, which enables flying with any aircraft from anywhere at any time. MSFS 2024 offers a new mode, though, that's a bit more structured: Photography Mode. It will present various photography challenges all around the world, where you can fly to different locations and snap amazing shots-including wildlife photography-to provide you with a structured way to explore the planet.

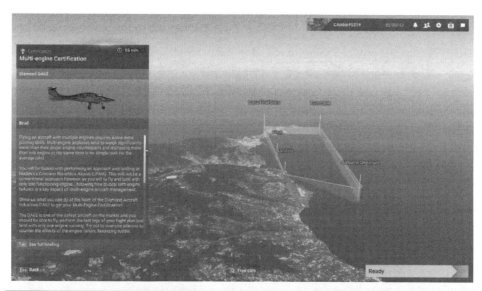

Overall, MSFS 2024 introduces a host of exciting new features and ways to explore the world. With a wide variety of new and updated aircraft, a dynamic career mode, and various flight planning tools, there's so much to look forward to. We're thrilled about this new chapter in digital aviation and can't wait to dive deeper into it with you. Make sure to check out our post on global release times so you can be ready to take off when MSFS 2024 launches.

CHAPTER 1
GETTING STARTED WITH MSFS 2024

Starting into home flight simulation can be fairly overwhelming initially-like trying to navigate through uncharted skies. Hardware options and software choices, not to mention learning virtually how to fly, abound. But don't sweat it; we have got your back. Whether you wish simply to enjoy some fun or to obtain flight training, this guidebook will get you up in the air without researching for days on end.

Here's what you'll find:

- A breakdown of flight simulator costs, from entry-level to high-end.
- The things you'll need to get your simulator up and running.
- Recommendations for controls and hardware, including computers.
- Guidance on how to choose the right flight simulation software.

Let's get you started on your flight simulation journey!

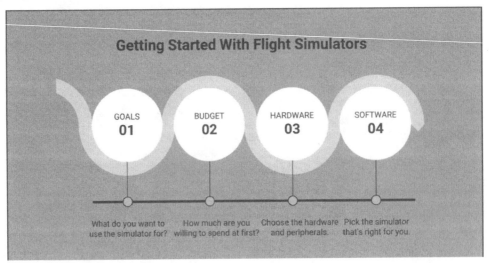

Flight simulator setups vary widely because they depend on your goals, budget, and the type of aircraft you want to simulate. Even the most elaborate and expensive setups typically begin modestly and grow over time.

We suggest taking the same approach.

First, you have to fix in your mind what your requirements, goals, and a tentative budget for flight simulators are. Once you're pretty clear about what your needs and expectations are and also the budget you can spend in the area, navigating options is far easier.

So, what are the essential components you'll need to get started with a flight simulator, no matter your budget or objectives?

WHAT YOU NEED FOR A FLIGHT SIMULATOR

To get started with a flight simulator, you'll need only a few items, which are surprisingly rather affordable. We will go into specific product recommendations later in the article.

PC / Xbox / Mac

First, you will need a device on which to run the simulator. While there are mobile options, such as the iPad, their performance is significantly worse compared to PCs, Xbox, or Macs, so we will focus on those platforms instead.

Joystick / Yoke + Throttle Quadrant

A joystick or yoke is necessary for flight control. While some joysticks have built-in throttles, adding a separate throttle quadrant can enhance your experience even further.

Keyboard / Mouse

A basic wireless keyboard and mouse are all you need for general navigation. Use the flight controls to fly and explore, and the mouse to interact with the cockpit.

Headset / Speakers

Audio is an important component in a flight simulation. Although there are some very impressive surrounds sound speakers, a good-quality headset, for about $60, provides excellent audio as well as a built-in microphone, which is a nice added bonus.

Inside a Real Flight Simulator Setup

With that said, let's look at how all these components come together in a high-end flight simulator setup and create an absolutely immersive cockpit experience.

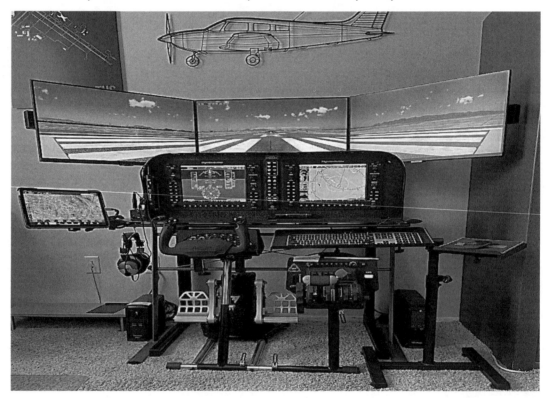

The Flight Simulator Setup by John Fralc

X-Plane 12 runs smoothly on an Apple Mac Studio equipped with the M1 Max chip in John's configuration. He uses ForeFlight on an iPad as his Electronic Flight Bag (EFB) for further capabilities. He utilizes PilotEdge to replicate authentic air traffic control (ATC) interactions. John uses Navigraph to access the most recent navigation charts for smooth flight planning and navigation.

Lessons Learned: The Serious Flight Sim Enthusiast

The owner of this advanced setup shared some key takeaways for anyone planning to build or upgrade their own flight simulator:

1. Future-Proof Your System:

A high-end PC might be a better option compared to a Mac for long-term performance. Whereas the Mac Studio works well with a single monitor, it shows its struggle with triple 4K monitors, which complicates further expansion with add-ons or resource-heavy aircraft.

2. Plan for Growth:

Consider your long-term goals in selecting your operating system. PCs have much more room for simulator enhancements and advanced configurations with the latest GPUs than Macs.

3. Monitor Mounting Tips:

A mount with full-axis adjustability is essential for achieving the right setup. If using a Sim-Lab triple monitor system, carefully measure your monitor's height requirements and ensure the mount's vertical legs are tall enough.

4. Enhance Realism with Custom Mods:

A few little things with custom modifications can sometimes make all the difference. In the case of the Honeycomb Bravo, a Cirrus throttle mod from ProDeskSim was attached, but one needs to make sure to utilize the newer version since the older version interfered with access to switches.

5. Lighting for Immersion:

These are strips of LED lights around the back side of the monitor, connected via USB, to enhance the experience of night flying through ambient background lighting. While this setup demonstrates what a home simulator is capable of, remember: small is okay. You can start off with an extremely minimal setup and continually add parts as your needs expand over time.

WHAT'S THE COST OF A HOME FLIGHT SIMULATOR?

Just around the corner, we will go through some costs and options so that you can plan your ideal setup.

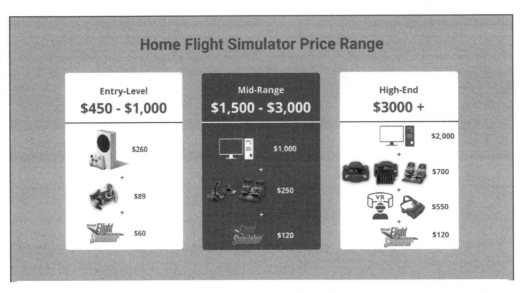

Before diving into your goals and ideal setup, let's break down the cost ranges for home flight simulators to help you plan your budget.

Entry-Level Setup: $450 – $1,000

- If you already own a gaming PC or Xbox, you can get started for as little as $149.
- Microsoft Flight Simulator: $60
- Joystick + Throttle Combo: $89
- For users without a computer, the Xbox Series S, $260, is a great option and powerful platform for less than one-third the cost of a gaming computer.

Mid-Range Setup: $1,500 – $3,000

- A mid-range setup provides major boosts in performance.
- Adding rudder pedals and a higher quality joystick and throttle ($250 for a combo) really elevates it.
- A gaming PC is required here, with $1,500 getting a very good one that will run most any simulator short of Virtual Reality (VR).

High-End Setup: $3,000+

- For pro users wanting to do VR or high effects work, a good starting point for a budget would be $4,000.

- High-end rigs are based on individual needs and can range from a multi-monitor setup to custom controls or a VR headset.

Start Small, Grow Over Time

No matter your budget, you don't have to go all-in immediately. Begin with a simple setup and gradually upgrade as you refine your goals.

Step 1: Define Your Goals

Now that you know the cost ranges, it's time to pinpoint your objectives.

Take a notepad and consider what you want to achieve with your simulator. Whether it's casual flying, training, or immersive realism, defining the purpose will keep you on track with the best setup.

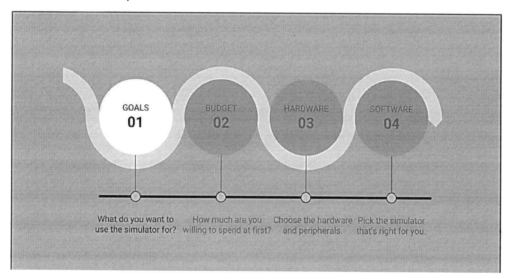

Home-based flight simulators generally fulfill one of three basic needs:

1. Recreational Flying: If you want to fly different aircraft in different scenarios, a flexible setup is what you need.

2. Real-Life Training: For training, you should try to set up a system as much like the airplane you fly as possible.

3. Combination of Both: Strike a balance by designing a setup similar to your real aircraft while allowing flexibility for other planes.

Step 2: Set Your Budget

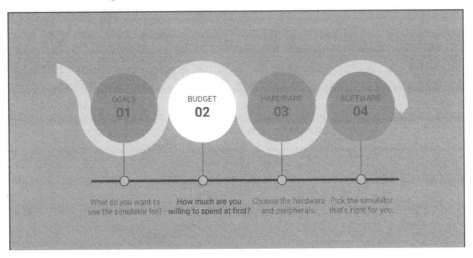

You don't have to spend a fortune to enjoy flight simulation. You can start with an initial budget that fits your needs since you can upgrade over time.

Step 3: Choose Your Hardware

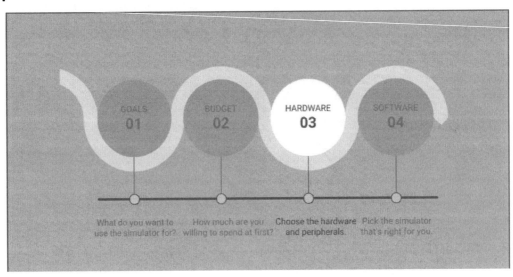

With your budget and goals in mind, here's what you'll need to get started:

Device: PC, Mac, or Xbox

Display: Monitor or TV

Controls: Joystick, yoke, and throttle

Optional: Rudder pedals-highly recommended

Audio: Headset or speakers

PC, MAC, OR XBOX: WHICH SHOULD YOU CHOOSE?

PC: The best choice for power, flexibility, and future upgrades. PCs are ideal for using third-party add-ons and online Air Traffic Control networks. If you want a system that grows with you, a PC is the way to go.

Xbox: The Xbox Series S or X is great for beginners, offering great performance at a lower price. However, it's less customizable and only supports Microsoft Flight Simulator.

Mac: Although Macs are not as popular among flight simulator users, they can run X-Plane without problems. If you already have a Mac and do not want to purchase new hardware, this is a good starting point.

Choose the platform that best aligns with your goals and budget, keeping in mind long-term possibilities.

WHAT'S THE BEST FLIGHT SIMULATOR FOR YOU?

The Everlasting Question: Which Flight Simulator is Right for You?

There have always been, until now, two reigning monarchs over civilian skies, namely:
- X-Plane
- Microsoft Flight Simulator (MSFS)

Regarding military aviation, there has only ever been one clear winner in town - that's DCS World., giving a whole different meaning to fighter jet aviation among others.

Microsoft Flight Simulator (MSFS)

MSFS is currently the most used and visually impressive flight simulator. It has been in a process of improvement in terms of reliability and features since its release, which has secured its position as the number one choice for many. Here's why MSFS shines: Unmatched Graphics: Leveraging satellite imagery and real-world 3D visuals in select areas, MSFS delivers breathtakingly realistic environments.

Immersive Audio: Clear and realistic sound effects make you feel truly inside the cockpit.

Thriving Community: Backed by Microsoft and a huge global community, this simulator keeps evolving with constant updates and innovations.

Thanks to its cutting-edge technology and ongoing support, Microsoft Flight Simulator is set to remain the favorite choice for years to come.

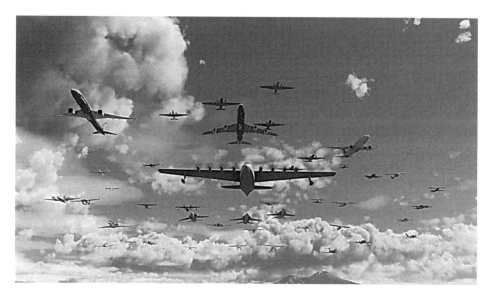

Microsoft Flight Simulator isn't without its challenges. Since its launch, it has faced notable reliability and performance issues. While many of these problems have been resolved and significant improvements made, MSFS still doesn't match the consistency of its main competitor, X-Plane.

Flight Model Realism: While the new MSFS has a remarkable flight model that is way beyond earlier versions, X-Plane is still ahead in the accuracy and realism of the flight dynamics.

Customization: MSFS is less flexible than X-Plane. If you fly a specific aircraft and use specific avionics in real life and want to exactly simulate those, then you will want to research carefully. Often, X-Plane has more options, and if your simulation needs are very specific, it's going to be the better choice.

While MSFS excels in graphics and audio, X-Plane remains the go-to for those prioritizing realism and adaptability.

X-Plane is widely regarded as the most realistic, customizable, and reliable flight simulator, which is why it's used in professional training setups. If you have a unique, custom avionics panel in real life, X-Plane lets you design and install it exactly how you want.

However, it does not have the graphic and terrain detail as Microsoft Flight Simulator. This will make navigation visually more difficult, but for IFR flying, this doesn't make it less effective.

DCS WORLD

DCS World is a combat flight simulator that allows you to experience military aviation including high-performance fighter jets. Given the complexity of flying such aircraft, it is less of a surprise that many DCS flyers are real-life pilots. You can learn to fly a simulator using DCS, but it is a better idea to learn basic flight skills in MSFS or XPlane and then move on to DCS. Fair warning: DCS is addictively entertaining!

Choosing Flight Simulator Controls

When choosing the right joystick or throttle for your flight simulator, here's what to consider:

Aircraft Type: Does your preferred aircraft use a joystick or yoke? If so, choose that kind of control, as it will be used most frequently.

Variety of Aircraft: If you are going to fly different kinds of planes, including helicopters, then a joystick is a good choice.

Button Needs: If you need a whole lot of buttons for intricate moves, say, in a military jet, go for a throttle or joystick with ample buttons.

Following are some recommended controls:

- Honeycomb Flight Controls (available for Xbox, too)
- Thrustmaster T.1600M FCS HOTAS
- Logitech G Flight Controls
- Thrustmaster T-Flight HOTAS One (Xbox-compatible)
- Logitech Extreme 3D Pro

Which Monitor Should I Buy for Flight Simulators?

You don't need an expensive monitor to fly in a simulator. Resolution and refresh rate are what matters:

Resolution: Higher resolution (4K or 1440p) means more detail, but requires a powerful PC.

Refresh Rate: Higher refresh rate (144Hz or 240Hz) means smoother visuals, but your PC needs to support it.

For the best balance, consider a 4K or 1440p monitor with a 60Hz refresh rate. A screen size of 27-32 inches will do nicely if you want the most sharpness. Consider three monitors or an ultrawide for the best immersion.

Headset Suggestions

Good headphones can enhance realism. A wired headset like the **HyperX Cloud II** (~$70) offers great value. If your budget allows, go for a wireless headset for freedom of movement, or invest in a **surround sound system** (though it might disturb your neighbors).

Do I Need Head Tracking or VR?

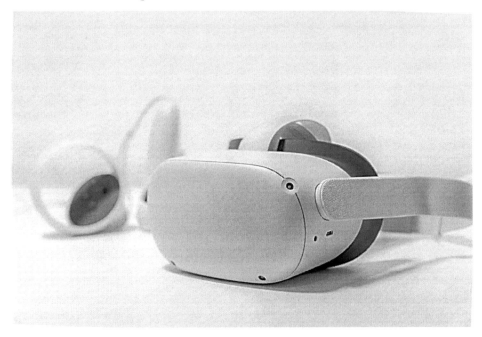

Head tracking and VR can boost immersion but aren't necessary:

Head Tracking: Useful for free movement in the cockpit, especially in military or VFR flying.

VR: A 3D experience that's ideal for depth perception and immersion.

IFR flights-in the clouds-do not require head tracking or VR. It is advisable to start with a standard monitor and then add head tracking or VR later.

ADVANCED AVIONICS SETUPS

If you want to enhance your flight simulator experience, adding physical buttons, knobs, and switches can go a long way. Fiddling with radios or GPS by mouse is frustrating and slow, but with the right panels, you will be able to interact with your simulator just like you would in a real aircraft, helping you build muscle memory.

For those flying on the G1000 we have a comprehensive guide to G1000 hardware panels and controls, and here are two popular options you can take your avionics setup to the next level with RealSimGear and with Air Manager:

RealSimGear - from single-product G1000 standalone panels, all the way up to more advanced, full Cirrus cockpit setups. Their systems go together relatively easily and customer service is very good.

Air Manager enables you to show your own aircraft panels on external monitors. This makes interacting with avionics such as the G1000 very easy if you have a touchscreen. It is a bit more technical to set up.

Another helpful tool is the Knobster, which, for many pilots, is used in combination with Air Manager. This small device enables you to control knobs on your avionics panel without using a mouse, and it's also useful for VR flying where the use of a mouse is not possible.

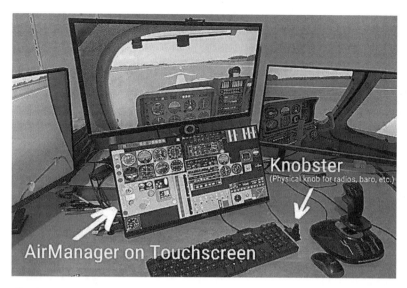

For a more realistic arrangement, Logitech also provides independent panels made for particular purposes like radios and autopilot.

All things considered, a home flight simulator can astonishingly mimic the actual flying experience provided you're prepared to put in the time and money.

SYSTEM REQUIREMENTS AND INSTALLATION

Microsoft Flight Simulator 2024 is coming out on November 19th, and it will be one of the most resource-intensive games in the market. While the minimum and recommended specs of the game are achievable by many gamers, running this game at the highest settings definitely requires a powerful machine.

Thankfully, Chillblast makes building gaming PCs for such demands its specialty. Whether you're after a flagship to max out 4K and ray tracing or a more budget-friendly option to deliver smooth 1080p gameplay, we have the right custom-built PC for your needs.

Let's delve into the system requirements for Microsoft Flight Simulator 2024 and find you the perfect Chillblast PC.

System requirements

Component	Minimum requirements	Recommended requirements	Ideal requirements
CPU	AMD Ryzen 5 2600X or Intel Core i7-6800K	AMD Ryzen 7 2700X or Intel Core i7-10700K	AMD Ryzen 9 7900X or Intel Core i7-14700K
Graphics	AMD Radeon RX 5700 or NVIDIA GeForce GTX 970	AMD Radeon RX 5700XT or NVIDIA GeForce RTX 2080	AMD Radeon RX 7900XT or NVIDIA GeForce RTX 4080
RAM	16GB	32GB	64GB
VRAM	4GB	8GB	12GB
Storage	50GB	50GB	50GB
Bandwidth	10Mbps	50 Mbps	100 Mbps
Operating System	Windows 10 with the latest update	Windows 10 with the latest update	Windows 10 with the latest update

MINIMUM SYSTEM REQUIREMENTS

CPU: AMD Ryzen 5 2600X, Intel Core i7-6800K, or better

RAM: 16GB

Graphics: AMD Radeon RX 5700, NVIDIA GeForce GTX 970, or better

VRAM: 4GB

Storage: 50GB

Bandwidth: 10 Mbps

Operating System: Windows 10 latest update

The minimum system requirements of Microsoft Flight Simulator 2024 are quite within the reach of most gamers. The specified CPUs are several years old and were mid-range upon release, so most modern PCs—especially gaming ones—should easily surpass this requirement. Similarly, 16GB of RAM has been a common standard in gaming PCs for several years. The recommended graphics cards are a bit more current, but still represent achievable performance targets. Indeed, according to the most recent Steam hardware survey, over 50% of respondents make use of a graphics card at least as powerful as the AMD Radeon RX 5700 or NVIDIA GeForce GTX 970.

For that matter, this game requires an uninterrupted and stable internet connection that's essential to avoid all sort of troubles with DRM but it is worth mentioning that Microsoft Flight Simulator deploys real-time weather and cloud processing to pump out the ultimate gameplay moments. It uses modest bandwidth of 10mbps - relatively modest, given that the average UK internet speed is now over 70 Mbps and 99.7 percent of homes have access to at least 10 Mbps.

Also, though Windows 10 is currently supported, official support, including security updates, will end in October 2025, so you should plan to upgrade to Windows 11 by then.

According to Microsoft, these minimum specs will let you run the game at 1080p with a 70% resolution scale, targeting 30 frames per second with all settings on low.

EXPLORING THE GAME INTERFACE

Best Gaming PC for Microsoft Flight Simulator 2024

If your current PC doesn't meet the minimum requirements for Microsoft Flight Simulator 2024 or you're thinking of building or buying a new gaming PC to fully enjoy this highly anticipated game, Chillblast has got you covered. We specialize in efficient, high-performance yet affordable gaming PCs, and we have several options that just fit budding flight simulation enthusiasts.

The best system we can recommend to run the newest Microsoft Flight Simulator is the Jetson Ryzen 5 RTX 4060 mid-tower gaming PC. With this computer, you can experience great game performance, even above the minimum requirements of the game, at a more budget-friendly price. We don't want you playing on low settings just to make the game playable.

Inside the Jetson PC, find the AMD Ryzen 5 7600 CPU: one of the top options available, touting six cores, 12-thread support, and high clock speeds that provide incredible performance while keeping cool and quiet. Paired with it, the build includes 16GB of fast DDR5 RAM and the GeForce RTX 4060 graphics card with 8GB of VRAM—double the minimum requirement for the game—and full support for the latest NVIDIA upscaling technology, including frame generation in supported games.

You'll also get a 1TB SSD for fast storage, built-in Wi-Fi and Gigabit Ethernet support, all nestled in a sleek DeepCool CH370 case. A whole package for an affordable price.

RECOMMENDED SYSTEM REQUIREMENTS

CPU: AMD Ryzen 7 2700X, Intel Core i7-10700K or better

RAM: 32GB

Graphics: AMD Radeon RX 5700XT, NVIDIA GeForce RTX 2080 or better

VRAM: 8GB

Storage: 50GB

Bandwidth: 50 Mbps

Operating System: Windows 10 (latest update)

The recommended system requirements push things further, but they're still achievable for many gamers. These CPUs and graphics cards were high-end when they launched, but they're now older models. However, Microsoft Flight Simulator is very demanding on your CPU, so it's important to have a processor with plenty of cores. Even a fast six-core CPU might struggle to keep up.

The suggested 32GB of RAM may be a reach for some, considering most PCs use 16GB. Luckily, RAM is one of the easiest and most economical upgrades you can make in your system. If you simply want more memory, it's easy to swap in your current RAM with a faster, higher-capacity kit.

The 50 Mbps bandwidth recommendation is a big jump, but it's still fairly reasonable for most gamers, especially in the UK, where the average internet speed is above this. Just be aware that other devices using the internet, such as streaming services, may slow things down while playing.

Meeting these specs will allow you to play the game at 1440p with high settings, though expect frame rates around 30 FPS.

Best Prebuilt PC for Microsoft Flight Simulator 2024

If you're looking to play at 1440p and your current PC doesn't meet the recommended requirements, we have just the thing: the Albatross Core i5 RTX 4070 SUPER gaming PC. This custom build is an absolute powerhouse for stunning 1440p visuals and higher frame rates.

Core: At its core, the Intel Core i5-14500 CPU is made of 14 cores and 20 threads, offering very good multi-threaded performance without going overboard with more expensive higher-end options. This processor is coupled with 32GB of ultra-fast DDR5 RAM to harness the full power of the powerful CPU.

The GeForce RTX 4070 SUPER with 12GB of VRAM easily surpasses the recommended requirements and provides great future-proofing for more demanding games. It outperforms older GPUs, like the RTX 3090, and supports NVIDIA DLSS and frame generation, which can greatly improve frame rates in supported games.

Ideal System Requirements for Microsoft Flight Simulator 2024

For those who want to enjoy Microsoft Flight Simulator 2024 at 4K Ultra settings with fluid framerates, Microsoft has unveiled "Ideal" system requirements. These are designed to achieve a framerate of around 40-50 FPS, with future optimizations possibly pushing it closer to 60 FPS.

At 4K Ultra, the game requires serious hardware: The recommended processors are some of the fastest on the market, with only a few more expensive variants outpacing them. It's also the first game to recommend 64GB of RAM, although Microsoft says the game won't actually use that much. The 64GB will guarantee 32GB is always free for the game, while the remainder is used by background tasks.

The graphics cards required are high-end models, just one step below the top-tier options. Unless you've recently purchased a flagship gaming PC, older hardware likely won't meet these demands.

Best Gaming PC for Microsoft Flight Simulator 2024

If you want to run Microsoft Flight Simulator 2024 with all settings cranked up and frame rates of over 60 FPS, this is the exact gaming PC you need: the Thunderbolt Ryzen 7 RTX 4080 SUPER Gaming PC. It is more than enough for perfect gameplay-it actually goes above and beyond the needed specs, giving truly incredible performance for gamers.

It features at its core an AMD Ryzen 7800X3D with eight cores and 3D V-Cache, capable of handling even the most demanding games with ease. The PC is equipped with 64GB of ultra-fast DDR5 memory and 2TB of high-speed SSD storage to make sure performance and ample space are available for all your games and applications.

The **GeForce RTX 4080 SUPER is** the standout feature of this build. With 16GB of VRAM and all the CUDA cores needed for top-tier gaming performance, this GPU is designed to push frame rates well above 60 FPS in Microsoft Flight Simulator 2024. Plus, with support for DLSS 3 and frame generation, it maximizes the game's performance and visual quality, delivering an incredible 4K experience with ultra-settings.

Connecting Peripherals: Joysticks, Yokes, and VR

How to Install OpenXR and Enable VR in Microsoft Flight Simulator

Installation of OpenXR

For Windows Mixed Reality Headsets:

If one uses a Windows Mixed Reality headset, there is nothing to be done. Your Microsoft Flight Simulator should function well with it.

For Non-WMR Headsets:

If using a non-WMR HMD (Oculus), then you must opt into the Oculus Rift Public Test Channel to access OpenXR. You do that here: [Oculus Rift Public Test Channel] (https://support.oculus.com/200468603765391).

In order for Flight Simulator to access your Oculus headset through OpenXR, you need to specify the location of the OpenXR runtime on your computer by editing the registry:

1. Right-click on the Start menu and click Run.

2. In the text box, type regedit (without quotes), and press Enter to launch the Registry Editor.

3. Navigate to:

`HKEY_LOCAL_MACHINE\\SOFTWARE\\Khronos\\OpenXR\\1`

4. Locate the ActiveRuntime section, and edit its value with the path from your platform-the default is:

`C:\\Program Files\\Oculus\\Support\\oculus-runtime\\oculus_openxr_64.json`

5. Now close the Registry Editor.

Your Oculus headset should now be configured for VR in Microsoft Flight Simulator.

How to Enable VR in Microsoft Flight Simulator

1. Launch Microsoft Flight Simulator in desktop mode first.

2. Turn on your VR headset application.

3. Launch Microsoft Flight Simulator and wear your headset.

4. Now, to enable VR mode, use the assigned VR command within the game settings, which is located under Options > General > VR Mode. Alternatively, you can click the VR button within that very same tab labeled VR Mode.

You are now ready to experience VR in Microsoft Flight Simulator!

CHAPTER 2
BASICS OF FLIGHT SIMULATION

Flight simulators are a safe, virtual environment in which pilots can enhance their skills and improve flying abilities. These simulators will simulate real-life flight dynamics and offer a range of aircraft models to suit the different training needs. They serve purposes ranging from basic flight training to advanced operational practice.

A flight simulator includes, but is not limited to, a detailed cockpit, flight instruments, and controls that realistically approximate the experience of piloting an actual aircraft. Using such systems, pilots can practice key maneuvers, such as takeoffs, landings, and navigation. In addition, simulators are necessary to train for emergency procedures- such as an engine or instrument failure.

They also help pilots get familiar with the aircraft they will be flying and the airports to which they will fly. Overall, flight simulators are a real treasure; they let pilots sharpen their skills and dive deeper into aviation's technical aspects.

Overview of Basics of Flight Simulator

Flight simulators are critical in pilot training, allowing them to practice their skills safely, which are then directly applicable in the field. The continuous evolution of these flight simulators has made them much more advanced, with better graphics and physically based flight models. This article examines some of the basic features of a flight simulator and how these tools have been applied to pilot training.

Simulators can be categorized as either basic or advanced. Basic simulators are designed to teach the fundamentals of flight, such as how to understand aircraft controls and the basic principles of flight. These systems generally feature simple instrument panels, controls, and visuals that simulate standard flight scenarios. They are often used for pre-flight briefings and helping pilots become acquainted with the aircraft they'll be operating.

The state-of-the-art flight simulator represents completely different dimensions, mimicking very closely the real-world environment of an aircraft. Such a simulator provides realistic graphics, complex control systems, and flight models based on applied physics. Such simulators are used to train a pilot in flying under IFR, bad weather conditions, emergency procedures, or system failure scenarios.

Flight simulators are programs designed to simulate the conditions of flying an aircraft. While they are primarily applied in the aviation industry for purposes of training pilots, they serve entertainment and educational purposes as well. They offer a safe and economic way for pilots to practice different maneuvers, procedures, and handling techniques without the real dangers associated with flight.

There are mainly two types of flight simulators: static and dynamic. Static simulators are normally used within the classroom environment, while dynamic simulators are higher-order systems that offer realistic cockpit environments. Both are designed for detailed simulations of a variety of aircraft and flying conditions.

The main components composing the parts of a flight simulator are a computer generating the flight environment, including terrain, weather, and other conditions; a visual display depicting the movement of the aircraft; a control system to steer the aircraft; and a sound system imitating real-life audio cues.

Simulators can model a wide range of aircraft-from small propeller planes to large commercial jets-and can mimic many different weather conditions: clouds, snow, turbulence, and fog. Pilots use simulators to practice such varied skills as takeoffs and landings, aerobatics, and emergency procedures, like the failure of an engine or cabin pressure, and difficulties with navigation.

Flight simulators also play a role in evaluating pilot performance by assessing reaction times, decision-making abilities, accuracy, and overall skills. This feedback helps pilots refine their performance and improve their abilities.

In addition to training, flight simulators are also popular for entertainment. Many people enjoy using flight simulation games on personal computers, allowing them to explore different aircraft and environments interactively.

In the end, flight simulators remain an essential part of pilots' training and entertaining activities, which offer realistic scenarios in enhancing their skills and having experiences.

1. Flight simulators are a vital resource for pilots at all levels of experience. They offer a realistic and controlled environment for pilots to refine their skills safely. Used for decades in training, simulators can replicate various aircraft, environments, and flight conditions, benefiting pilots in both commercial and military settings to maintain proficiency and enhance their flying experience.

2. Flight simulators are designed to closely simulate actual flight. Advanced software allows them to simulate the aircraft's behavior under various conditions and the environment in which the aircraft is operating. The simulator's cockpit mirrors that of a real aircraft, complete with control panels, instruments, and other features to provide an authentic feel.

3. Simulators are used by pilots to enhance their performance regarding navigation, communication, instrument flying, and situational awareness. They can practice takeoffs, landings, and emergency maneuvers under different conditions, allowing them to gain the practical experience needed for success in real flights.

4. Flight simulators also prepare pilots for the demands of airline operations: essential procedures such as communicating with air traffic control, navigating unfamiliar terrain, and handling various weather conditions. Regular simulator sessions keep pilots sharp and ready for whatever they may face in the skies.

5. Flight simulators are used by aircraft manufacturers in testing new aircraft designs and configurations before manufacture. Simulators enable manufacturers to check the aircraft's performance in various situations to ensure it meets safety and performance standards before actually being built, thus making the aircraft much safer and more reliable.

6. Simulators play an important role in pilots' lives, from beginners to experienced ones. They give a comfortable environment for practicing skills and simulating real-life situations that would make the pilots more proficient and prepared for any situation. They are also useful for aircraft manufacturers in testing the safety and reliability of newly designed aircraft.

7. Flight simulators have been invaluable in the training and development of pilots. They keep pilots sharp and hone their skills by allowing them to practice a wide range of procedures and scenarios, which enhances their flying experience and better equips them for in-flight challenges.

8. Basic to commercial, military, and general aviation, flight simulators are invaluable for pilots honing their craft. Simulating several types of aircraft in numerous flight circumstances, these tools help keep any pilot razor-sharp in preparation for flying.

9. Flight simulators also play an important role for manufacturers in testing and refining new aircraft designs before they reach production lines, a process that helps ensure safety and reliability. For this reason, combined with its importance in pilot training, simulators have become a cornerstone of modern aviation.

10. Simulators are an essential asset to pilots of all levels. They offer a safe, realistic environment to practice and hone their flying skills under various conditions and aircraft. Regular use of simulators can keep pilots ready to face any new challenge arising from their experience in the skies.

UNDERSTANDING AERODYNAMICS IN THE VIRTUAL WORLD

More OEMs are adopting virtual technology to validate performance, particularly for structural and aerodynamic tests. Virtual Wind Tunnel offers a variety of possibilities to efficiently conduct wind tunnel analysis of aircraft structures and allows for both steady-state and transient studies at faster rates with precision.

Today, design exploration and optimization have gone widespread across industries such as aerospace, automotive, and heavy industries with the help of virtual validation. High-performance computing platforms aid engineers in accelerating simulations and fine-tuning designs. Under aerodynamics, it was possible to analyze airflow only around the fuselage and wing but now also around nacelles and air intakes, taking virtual validation to cargo aircraft and drones.

Virtual aerodynamics validation in the fifth generation of fighter aircraft is crucial, especially toward the features of stealth, RCS, and complex air intake design. Virtual validation allows designers to investigate the effects of design features like the separation between fuselage and engine intake and the performance evaluation by using the parametric CFD model.

As fighter aircraft evolve, virtual validation supports quick maneuvers and design modifications. For naval versions of fighter aircraft-where modifications like heavier underbellies or altered front cones are required-virtual aerodynamics validation helps designers optimize before committing to physical prototypes, especially when testing facilities are not available.

Looking ahead, the shift toward zero-emission flights and alternative propulsion systems, including hybrid technologies, is going to further increase the need for virtual validation in aerodynamics. For commercial aircraft, this involves wing design optimization, nacelle shapes, and noise-reducing features. In defense, virtual validation aids in the design of multi-role fighters, balancing stealth and aerodynamics while optimizing weapon bay designs. In the end, it is powerful algorithms and simulations that let designers gain valuable insight before any physical prototype takes to the sky.

Microsoft Flight Simulator 2024, or MSFS 2024 for short, is the highly anticipated sequel of the 2020 version. It launches on November 19, 2024, and is claimed to be a significant technological leap forward, promising to immerse flying simulation enthusiasts in their games even more. Already, it has been causing a stir within the community.

Microsoft Flight Simulator 2024 offers a new flight activity system beyond simple free flight. Realistic, structured aviation missions are offered in cooperation with real-life fire departments, search and rescue teams, and coast guards to authentically replicate their operations in the game.

Players can now play the roles of aerial firefighting, medical evacuations, cargo transport, VIP charters, and air racing for a more realistic feel. Missions are designed with input from professionals for authenticity, adding both realism and an educational element for those interested in aviation.

MSFS 2024 makes huge steps regarding simulation and technology, providing major updates to the core engine with a new multithreaded physics and aerodynamics system. Such a development allows for the enhancement of flight dynamics to make aircraft more realistic when reacting to the forces of lift, drag, and turbulence that they may encounter.

Additionally, it features optimization in performance due to a "thin client" architecture that incorporates cloud streaming. This lowers the requirement for local storage and raises efficiency with the streaming of high-quality graphics and detailed environments directly to player devices. The new system also makes for smoother performance on a wide variety of hardware configurations, though its full impact will be clear after it is released and further testing.

What makes Microsoft Flight Simulator 2024 very special, though, is that it'll be cross-platform, offering the game to more players and enthusiasts alike. The different hardware owners will get a chance to enjoy the game with the release of Microsoft Flight Simulator 2024 on Windows PCs and Xbox Series X|S consoles. By optimizing the game for high-end gaming PCs and new consoles alike, Microsoft warrants the best possible gaming experience across all platforms.

MSFS 2024 will also be available in the Xbox Game Pass service from day one for console, PC, and cloud. What that means is that subscribers will have a way to play at no extra cost over their subscription-a lot more affordable than what entry might cost them. The ability to use cloud gaming further opens avenues for people on multiple devices, which independently might not have the grunt to handle this pretty graphically intensive simulator.

Community concerns about compatibility with existing add-ons and the transition from the 2020 version have been heard, as Microsoft has ensured that most add-ons for the previous version will work in MSFS 2024. Players can continue to fly their favorite aircraft, scenery, and third-party enhancements without needing to repurchase or wait for updates.

In addition, MSFS 2024 will retain the use of a community folder for add-ons created by players. This feature not only preserves the work of modders and developers but also makes it easier for players to manage and transfer their existing add-ons to the new simulator. The result of this integration is smoothness in transitioning and fostering continued innovation within the flight simulation community.

Microsoft Flight Simulator 2024 has generated some buzz with its possible career mode, although details are not yet clear. The community is expecting a well-structured career progression in the game, enabling players to go through stages of an aviation career, such as obtaining pilot licenses and completing various missions in commercial aviation, cargo transport, and search and rescue operations. This mode could offer a variety of challenges, making the experience more engaging and educational.

Another expected addition is the ability to use pilot avatars, enabling the creation and customization of characters that can be used within career modes and missions. More interactive ground operations, such as refueling, loading cargo, and boarding passengers, could also be added to the game, even allowing players to play the role of ground crew.

Visually, MSFS 2024 introduces significant enhancements, especially in scenery and building models. Improved terrain data and photogrammetry deliver more detailed and accurate landscapes, while buildings now feature better textures and realistic architectural details. These upgrades, particularly in urban areas, create a stunningly realistic environment, setting a new visual standard for flight simulation.

AIRCRAFT CATEGORIES: FROM PROPS TO JETS

The differences among aircraft category, class, and type sometimes seem foggy for newcomers in aviation. This article will explain each of these terms and describe how they differ from each other. You will clearly understand, by the end, what sets each apart and why it is important that you understand it.

Whether you are a budding pilot, an aviation enthusiast, or simply curious, this article will walk you through the important concepts. Before we begin, let's point out that "category" can refer to the pilot, the aircraft, or an instrument approach. We will discuss all three definitions, starting with those related to pilot certification.

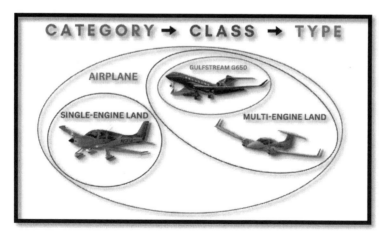

Here's a breakdown, simplified, of how aircraft are categorized:

Category: This is the major class into which an aircraft would fall, considering the way an aircraft is used and the mission it is to perform: examples are airplanes, helicopters or rotorcraft, gliders, and balloons.

Class: A smaller class within a category, focused more on design and performance, such as single-engine or multi-engine airplane classes.

Type: Identifies the specific make and model of an aircraft, for example, Boeing 737 or Airbus A320. Pilots require a "type rating" to fly jets or aircraft over 12,500 pounds.

What is an Aircraft Category?

Aircraft categories are broad groups that classify aircraft by their purpose and how they operate. These classifications are recognized by organizations like the FAA and serve to organize aircraft with similar characteristics.

Here are the main categories:

Airplane: Fixed-wing, engine-powered aircraft that achieve lift through their wings.

Glider: Aircraft designed to fly without an engine, relying on air currents for lift.

Rotorcraft: Aircraft, such as helicopters, that use rotating blades for lift.

Lighter-Than-Air: Aircraft, such as balloons or airships, that remain aloft by using lighter-than-air gas.

Powered Lift: Aircraft with vertical takeoff capabilities, such as tiltrotor planes.

These categories help outline a framework as to how different types of aircraft fly and are utilized.

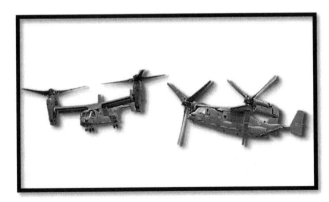

Powered Lift

Powered lift aircraft, like the Bell Boeing V-22 Osprey, are the real utility players. Powered lift aircraft can take off and land vertically. They derive their lift from either propellers or thrust, provided by an engine during low-speed flight, switching to fixed wings for high-speed efficient flight.

Powered Parachute

A powered parachute is pretty much what the name implies - a person in a harness below a parachute with an attached engine and propeller that provides forward motion. Technically it's an aircraft with an engine and flexible wing that needs to be moving to take off.

Weight-Shift Control

This is a type of powered aircraft, such as an ultralight trike, which possesses a pivoting wing, by adjusting the center of gravity controls the pitch and roll. Unlike traditional aircraft, it doesn't have conventional control surfaces like ailerons or elevators.

Rocket

Rockets are aircraft that are powered by expanding gases produced by self-contained fuel. They do not require external air intake to generate thrust. You will not find rockets on any private pilot certificate, but they are still considered aircraft.

Aircraft Class Explained

Aircraft class further sub-divides broad categories into smaller groups based on design and performance. It lumps similar aircraft together within a category.

For example, the airplane category is further broken down into these classes:
- Single-Engine Land
- Single-Engine Sea
- Multi-Engine Land
- Multi-Engine Sea

These categories and classes together then help to define what kind of aircraft a pilot is certified to fly.

Aircraft Categories, Classes, and Types Here's a simplified breakdown of aircraft categories, classes, and types defined by the FAA:

Aircraft Categories and Classes

Each category of aircraft groups similar types based on design or use. The full list follows with their specific classes:

Airplane
- Single-Engine Land
- Single-Engine Sea
- Multi-Engine Land
- Multi-Engine Sea

Glider
- No additional classes

Rotorcraft
- Helicopter
- Gyroplane

Lighter-Than-Air
- Airship
- Balloon

Powered Lift
- No additional classes

Powered Parachute
- Powered Parachute Land
- Powered Parachute Sea

Weight-Shift Control
- Weight-Shift Control Land
- Weight-Shift Control Sea

Rocket
- No additional classes

What is an Aircraft Type?

An aircraft type denotes a specific make and model, such as a Boeing 737 or Airbus A320. It represents unique design and capabilities, and not just any pilot can fly them. For example,

For aircraft weighing over 12,500 pounds or any jet requires a type rating. That is an endorsement on the pilot's license indicating he or she has completed the necessary training for that specific aircraft.

Sometimes, one type rating applies to similar models of the same family provided that differences between them are not significant. For example, both the Beechcraft 1900D and 1900C have one type rating since both have similar handling and characteristics.

ALL MEANINGS OF "AIRCRAFT CATEGORY"

The term aircraft category** has several meanings depending on the context. Briefly, here's what they are:

1. Pilot Certification: General categories such as airplanes, gliders, or rotorcraft—already discussed.

2. Aircraft Certification: The classification of aircraft based on their size and capabilities- such as normal, utility, transport, aerobatic.

3. Instrument Approaches: Categorizes aircraft according to their landing performance by approach speeds (Categories A to E).

Aircraft Certification Categories

These are based on design and purpose of operation:

Standard Airworthiness Categories

- **Aerobatic:** Aircraft certificated for aerobatic flight, maximum 9 seats, 12,500 lbs.
- **Commuter**: Multi-engine props for up to 19 passengers (under 19,000 lbs).
- **Normal**: Non-aerobatic, carrying 9 or fewer passengers (max 12,500 lbs).
- **Transport**: Larger aircraft, categorized by engine type and seating.
- **Utility**: Limited aerobatics (max 9 seats, 12,500 lbs).

Special Airworthiness Categories

Experimental: Covers amateur-built, unmanned, or prototype aircraft.

Light Sport (LSA): Sport aircraft not in other categories.

Limited: Military aircraft adapted for civilian use.

Primary: Personal-use aircraft (not for hire).

Provisional: Temporary certifications (Class I for 24 months, Class II for 12 months).

Restricted: Specialized aircraft for tasks like agriculture or weather control.

Some aircraft, such as those in "Normal" or "Utility," may fall into different categories depending on weight and balance on a given flight.

Aircraft Approach Categories

These are a description of how an aircraft will perform on landings, based on Vref(1.3x the stalling speed in landing configuration):

- **Category A**: ≤ 90 knots (e.g., small single-engine planes).
- Category B: 91–120 knots (e.g., small multi-engine planes).
- **Category C**-121–140 kt. Examples include airliners.
- **Category D**-141–165 kt. Large, airliners or jets would fall into this category
- **Category E**- ≥166 kt. Examples might include jets, particularly military

Categories work to make landings by placing limitations on landing attempts in all categories.

Slower aircraft will afford great flexibility and tighter maneuvers such as those found within a Category A, for instance, whereas the speedsters-a Category D or Category E- will need some significant space and time over approach.

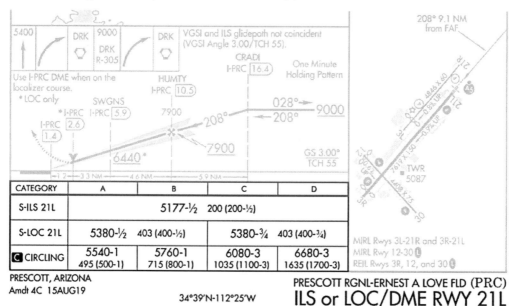

Approach categories are defined by performance and not by an aircraft's size, weight, or type. Thus, two very different aircraft could fall into the same category if their performance characteristics match. If a crew chooses to approach at a higher speed, the speed-related limitations for the corresponding approach category will apply. Notice, too, that decision altitude (DA) and minimum descent altitude (MDA) can vary between approach categories, further reflecting performance-based distinctions.

THE ROLE OF WEATHER AND NAVIGATION

Microsoft Flight Simulator 2024 enables you to adjust all sorts of settings to make flights as realistic as possible, including weather and time of day, factors that may affect flight paths and visibility, furthering your immersion. Free Flight mode gives you complete freedom in choosing an aircraft and flying over any location on Earth. Whether you want to explore Manhattan at night or see the Great Pyramids in a snowstorm, it's all possible. This guide will walk you through adjusting the weather and time settings, both before and during your flights.

How to Adjust Weather & Time of Day

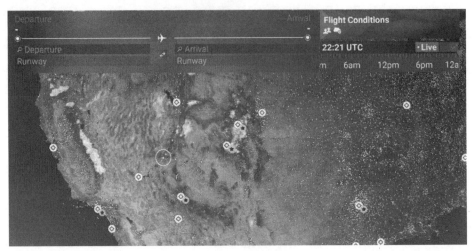

In Free Flight mode, you begin with a map of Earth where you choose your aircraft and plan a route. At the top-right side of the screen is a set of radio buttons to select Flight Conditions; a clock is located just below these. If the clock has "Live" selected it will display the current real-world time in your simulator. Click the selection to turn the "Live" setting off if that's not the time of day you want.

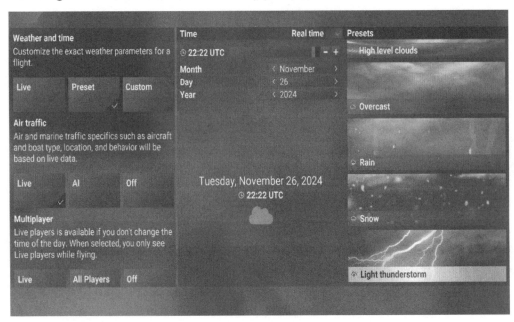

For further customization, open the Flight Conditions panel. Xbox users can do this by hitting Y. This will bring up the panel where you can change the weather and time settings:

Live Mode: Keeps real-world weather and time for the areas you're flying in. You can also roll the real-world weather back up to 24 hours while maintaining its accuracy.

Preset Mode: Provides several weathers preset scenarios and the capability for manual time setting.

Custom Mode: Provides detailed control with altitude-dependent weather, air pressure, humidity, lightning, snow coverage, and precipitation tunable.

Change of Weather/Time In-Flight

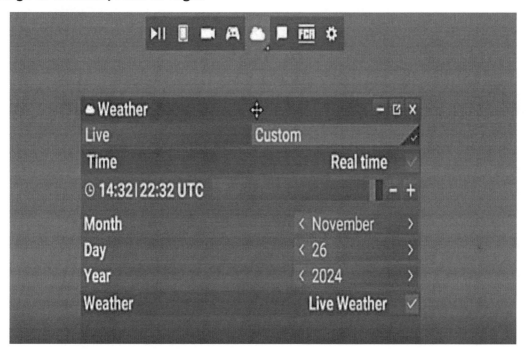

You can make all the above settings in flight.

- On PC, move your cursor to the top of the screen and click the small cloud icon.
- On Xbox, press RB + L3 to activate cursor mode, then click the weather icon.

Once you have opened the weather menu, feel free to change conditions according to your preference. Do note that changing the weather or time while in flight may result in slight delays in the simulation because of loading changes into Microsoft Flight Simulator 2024.

CHAPTER 3
SETTING UP FOR REALISM

Microsoft Flight Simulator 2024 pushes the envelope on realism, with even higher fidelity than its predecessor in 2020. It's a true technical tour de force, presenting the entire Earth in breathtaking detail. The aircraft and cockpits aren't just visually impressive-they're also highly functional and immersive. Mated with authentic flight physics, it's an unparalleled achievement in simulation gaming. While some quirks remain, no other game has yet attempted to model the entirety of the planet at this degree of accuracy.

That said, it wasn't all smooth sailing on launch. In fact, server issues prevented many-a-player, including yours truly, from getting into the game for a good while. Thankfully, these issues have been largely ironed out. But there are still minor quibbles, such as areas of incomplete high-res geometry, like the Grand Canyon. Disappointing as those launch-day frustrations were, the experience today is a much more silky-smooth one, and therefore easier to forgive the rough start.

It's also important to acknowledge that your experience will depend on your internet setup. Modern Flight Simulator relies heavily on streaming data, which means network quality matters. I've been fortunate to have gigabit wired internet and dedicated 200 GB on a fresh SSD for the game's rolling cache, which stores terrain data for frequently visited areas. Load times, even for a first launch, are significantly improved compared to FS2020. Microsoft recommends at least 100 Mbps for maximum settings, though I've found the game typically uses no more than 46 Mbps. Still, it's something players should keep in mind when setting up for the best experience.

Microsoft Flight Simulator 2024 is designed to engage three kinds of players: dedicated simmers seeking ultra-realistic experiences, gamers chasing rewards for completing challenges, and explorers eager to fly over iconic landmarks. I think I have a little of all three in me. I appreciate the little details of realism, get geeky seeing a flight under a beautifully recreated Golden Gate Bridge, and like progress-the numbers going up.

For simmers and sightseers, FS2024 delivers in spades. It's the career mode-a system designed to provide structure and goals-that feels a little light. I certainly enjoyed earning things like my IFR flight certification, or my certification to fly jet aircraft. The freelance pilot economy feels incredibly simplistic and grind-heavy. It takes hours of missions—like dropping skydivers or firefighting—on rented planes to earn enough to buy even the cheapest aircraft with most earnings lost to finder's fees. The variety keeps things fresh, but it never quite feels like running a small aviation business.

Visually, FS2024 is a stunner. Flying through gorgeous, lifelike clouds or exploring bespoke landmarks and airports is a real treat. From an altitude of 1,000 feet, it's easily one of the most beautiful games I've played. But on the ground, the immersion can vary. Rural and wilderness areas feel eerily accurate—walking through Divide, Colorado, for instance, was like stepping into my childhood. Urban areas, however, can look odd and surreal, and coastal regions suffer from static waves and unnatural riverbanks. These blemishes certainly stand in contrast to the otherwise sterling realism of the game, but it's hard not to be impressed by the outright audacity of mapping the entire planet.

To take full advantage of FS2024, you'll want a good internet connection, a decent GPU, and, if possible, a flight control peripheral. You don't need to break the bank; a relatively low-cost joystick like the Logitech Extreme 3D Pro, supplemented with a keyboard for additional controls, will serve nicely.

I tried flying using an Xbox controller for perhaps 12 hours, but the best I can say about the experience is that you might consider it if no other options are available. A general lack of fine-grained throttle control is relentless frustration and the tiny thumbstick makes every control surface much too sensitive. Holding the right angle for climbing left my hands cramped, and I had to fiddle with sensitivity settings for each plane just so I wouldn't crash upon takeoff and landing. And using just a mouse and keyboard? I wouldn't even want to think about it.

If hardcore simulation isn't your thing, there are plenty of options to tailor your experience. With all assists turned on, flying feels very arcade-like—too much so for my taste—but it's great to have the flexibility. On the flip side, you can immerse yourself in every detail, from completing pre-flight checklists to manually flipping cockpit switches before takeoff. The updated air traffic control system offers more depth than FS2020, though the robotic AI voices still leave much to be desired. With so many missions and airports, recording human voices for all of it probably wasn't practical, but the artificial tone does take away some of the realism.

FINAL DESTINATIONS

The variety of aircraft in the base edition of Flight Simulator is impressive, offering 70 options that range from commercial airliners and fighter jets to hot air balloons. Each one handles differently, presenting unique challenges that make every flight feel like learning the personality of a new companion. While helicopters never quite clicked for me, I've grown particularly fond of the rugged "taildragger" bush planes. These agile machines let me take off and land almost anywhere—like the middle of an open field in Africa.

Adding to the experience, many remote areas now feature migrating wildlife, with beautifully detailed and animated models borrowed from Planet Zoo. While the animals don't exhibit much behavior—you can walk right up to a polar bear or water buffalo without so much as a reaction—it's still a fun detail. Plus, it's a great excuse to use the game's robust photo tools. The new World Photographer mode, which tasks you with capturing images of various animals and landmarks, offers a relaxing diversion from the more structured career mode.

If you're looking to push your piloting abilities to the limit, Flight Simulator offers a variety of challenges with weekly leaderboards. These range from mastering tricky landings to adrenaline-fueled feats like flying an F-18 through the Grand Canyon while hugging the terrain at impossibly low altitudes—basically, some *Top Gun*-style action. While these challenges are exciting, they're definitely more intense and nerve-wracking than the other game modes.

Of course, no simulation is perfect, and FS2024 has its share of quirks and bugs. For instance, at some smaller procedurally-generated airports, my plane would sometimes spawn with a wing awkwardly stuck in a building, making takeoff impossible. Other times, I'd get penalized for infractions like using flaps at high speeds—even when the plane was stationary with the parking brake engaged. Though they are rare and generally, easily avoidable by simply selecting a different mission, they do get frustrating if or when they occur.

These minor hiccups hardly take away from what Flight Simulator 2024 achieves as a whole. It builds on the groundbreaking ambition of the 2020 version and elevates it, even if not everything it tries lands perfectly. At its core, the essence of what has made this franchise a favorite for decades is stronger than ever.

GRAPHICS AND PERFORMANCE OPTIMIZATION

You don't have to turn every setting to its maximum to enjoy great visuals in Microsoft Flight Simulator. After fiddling with the graphics settings, I was able to greatly increase frames-per-second while still enjoying great visuals and detailed terrain. The difference compared to running everything on Ultra was barely noticeable, but the smoother flying experience made it well worth it.

Note that this will be different in your system, depending on your hardware, and may further change with updates or optimizations by Asobo Studio. These results are based on an Intel Core i7-9750, RTX 2060 GPU with 6GB VRAM, 16GB of RAM, and a 512GB SSD.

To ensure that Microsoft Flight Simulator works optimally, follow these steps:

1. Update Your Operating System:

Ensure Windows 10 or Windows 11 is updated. Open the Start menu, go to Settings > Windows Update, and click Check for updates to install any pending updates.

2. Update Microsoft Store Apps:

Keep your Microsoft Store apps up to date. Launch the Microsoft Store, click on Library at the bottom left, then click Get updates at the top right. Install any available updates.

3. Disable Automatic Updates (Optional):

To avoid updates running in the background and affecting Flight Simulator's performance, disable automatic updates. Open Windows Update > Advanced options and toggle off the feature.

4. Keep Your GPU Drivers Up-to-Date:

Check that the driver is appropriate for your Graphics Processing Unit. Too old, and in some cases even very new drivers, may have effects on performance. Download the latest official driver for your NVIDIA GeForce or AMD Radeon graphics card from their respective websites.

- If you are using GeForce Experience, be aware that it may make changes to MSFS automatically without your intervention. To avoid this, at the point of installation, select Custom (Advanced) under Installation options, and uncheck GeForce Experience.
- Optionally, check Perform a clean installation to reset your Nvidia Control Panel (NCP) settings to default.

5. Optimize Nvidia Control Panel Settings:

After installing the driver, fine-tune the settings in Nvidia Control Panel as recommended for MSFS performance improvements.

By keeping your system and drivers up-to-date and carefully managing settings, you'll enjoy a smoother and more stable flight simulation experience.

Before launching Microsoft Flight Simulator, do a little tweaking in Windows 10 or 11 to improve performance and stability:

1. Enable Game Mode:

Game Mode optimizes system resources for gaming by reducing background tasks.

- Open the Start menu, go to Settings.
- In the search bar, type Game Mode, then enable it.
- Under Related settings, click Graphics > Change default graphics settings and ensure the following are ON:

- Hardware-accelerated GPU scheduling (HAGS).
- Optimizations for windowed games

2. Adjust Capture Settings:

- Use the search bar to find Capture settings.
- Turn Record what happened OFF to reduce unnecessary background activity.

3. Set Virtual Memory Manually:

Manually setting up Virtual Memory can prevent crash-to-desktop issues and stuttering.

- Open View advanced system settings via the Windows search bar.
- Under the Advanced tab, click Settings (under Performance).

In Performance Options, open the Advanced tab:

- Under Processor scheduling, select Programs and click Apply.
- Now, under Virtual Memory, click Change:
- Deselect Automatically manage paging file size for all drives.
- Give the drive letter where Windows is installed, usually C:.

In the Custom size option, set:

Initial size: 49152 MB

Maximum size: 49152 MB

- If you have 32GB or more RAM, select System managed size instead.
- click Set, then OK, and restart your computer.

These changes will help to enhance system performance, reduce crashes, and make MSFS run more smoothly.

It's time to further tune up graphics settings in Microsoft Flight Simulator to achieve the ultimate performance vs. visual balance. The following settings will be needed to achieve perfection under GENERAL OPTIONS:

1. Select the Display Mode:

- FULL SCREEN should be selected, of course.
- Check that Full Screen Resolution matches your native monitor resolution.
- For instance, if you are working with Full HD, select 1920x1080.
- With a 4K monitor, you may want 2560x1440 for sharper visuals; however, this may hit your frame rate.

2. Start with Global Rendering Quality:

- Set Global Rendering Quality to ULTRA to begin with to reset all the settings to their highest.
- Then, turn specific settings down to reach even smoother performance with high-quality views of visuals and terrain detail.

All these tweaks will result in giving you a great visual flying simulation game without compromising smooth flying gameplay.

CUSTOMIZING CONTROLS AND HOTKEYS

November 2024: A complete list of key binds and hotkeys for Microsoft Flight Simulator 2024, featuring search and filter options for easy navigation.

Categories:

- ☐ Autopilot
- ☐ Banner Hook
- ☐ Banner Pole
- ☐ Brakes
- ☐ Camera
- ☐ Camera (Cockpit)
- ☐ Camera (Drone)
- ☐ Camera (External)
- ☐ Camera (Photo Mode)
- ☐ Camera (Slew)
- ☐ Communications
- ☐ Developer Mode
- ☐ Firefighting
- ☐ Flight Control Surfaces
- ☐ Instruments
- ☐ Landing Gear
- ☐ Lights
- ☐ Miscellaneous
- ☐ Player Character
- ☐ Power Management
- ☐ Skydive System
- ☐ Tools
- ☐ VR

Action	Keyboard Command	Category
Zoom Out	SHIFT + U	Camera (Photo Mode)
Zoom In	SHIFT + O	Camera (Photo Mode)
Zoom External View	SHIFT + O	Camera (External)
Zoom Cockpit View	SHIFT + O	Camera (Cockpit)
Yaw Drone Right	L	Camera (Drone)
Yaw Drone Left	J	Camera (Drone)
VR - Toolbar Toggle	ALT + T	VR
VR - Camera Reset	SHIFT + VR	VR
VR - Activate/Deactivate VR Mode	CTRL + TAB	VR
VOR OBS	CTRL + 0	Instruments
Validate	ENTER	Developer Mode
Unzoom External View	SHIFT + U	Camera (External)
Unzoom Cockpit View	SHIFT + U	Camera (Cockpit)
Ungroup	CTRL + SHIFT + G	Developer Mode
Undo	CTRL + W	Developer Mode
Transponder	↓	Instruments
Translate Drone Up	E	Camera (Drone)
Translate Drone Right	D	Camera (Drone)
Translate Drone Left	A	Camera (Drone)
Translate Drone Forward	W	Camera (Drone)
Translate Drone Down	Q	Camera (Drone)
Translate Drone Backward	S	Camera (Drone)
Translate Cockpit View Right	SHIFT + D	Camera (Cockpit)
Translate Cockpit View Left	SHIFT + A	Camera (Cockpit)
Translate Cockpit View Forward	SHIFT + W	Camera (Cockpit)
Translate Cockpit View Backward	SHIFT + S	Camera (Cockpit)
Toggle Water Rudder	CTRL + /	Flight Control Surfaces
Toggle VFR Cockpit Mode	SHIFT + F10 ↓	Instruments
Toggle Taxi Ribbon	ALT + 3	Tools

- Toggle Taxi Ribbon: ALT + 3 (Tools)
- Toggle Tail Hook Handle: CTRL + / (Miscellaneous)
- Toggle Spray: Z (Firefighting)
- Toggle Smart Camera: CTRL + B (Camera)
- Toggle Slew Mode: SHIFT + Z (Camera - Slew)
- Toggle Sim Pause: SPACE (Developer Mode)
- Toggle Screen Narrator: ALT + Backspace (Tools)
- Toggle Run: SPACE (Player Character)
- Toggle Pushback: ALT + P (Tools)
- Toggle Pause: ESC (Tools)
- Toggle Parking Brakes: CTRL + SPACE (Brakes)
- Toggle Nameplates: ALT + 2 (Tools)
- Toggle Master Battery and Alternator: CTRL + Z (Instruments)
- Toggle Lead Pole: X (Banner Pole)
- Toggle Landing Ribbon: ALT + 4 (Tools)
- Toggle Landing Gear: / (Landing Gear)
- Toggle Landing Cockpit Mode: SHIFT + F11 (Instruments)
- Toggle Instrument View 9: SHIFT + NUM 9 (Camera - Cockpit)
- Toggle Instrument View 8: SHIFT + NUM 8 (Camera - Cockpit)
- Toggle Instrument View 7: SHIFT + NUM 7 (Camera - Cockpit)
- Toggle Instrument View 6: SHIFT + NUM 6 (Camera - Cockpit)
- Toggle Instrument View 5: SHIFT + NUM 5 (Camera - Cockpit)
- Toggle Instrument View 4: SHIFT + NUM 4 (Camera - Cockpit)
- Toggle Instrument View 3: SHIFT + NUM 3 (Camera - Cockpit)
- Toggle Instrument View 2: SHIFT + NUM 2 (Camera - Cockpit)
- Toggle Instrument View 10: SHIFT + NUM 0 (Camera - Cockpit)
- Toggle Instrument View 1: SHIFT + NUM 1 (Camera - Cockpit)
- Toggle IFR Cockpit Mode: SHIFT + F9 (Instruments)
- Toggle Headphone Simulation: ALT + H (Tools)
- Toggle Head Tracking: ALT + 7 (VR)
- Toggle Grapple Hook: Z (Banner Hook)
- Toggle G Limiter: Z (Instruments)
- Toggle Foreground Blur: 4 (Camera - Drone)
- Toggle Flight Assistant: ALT + 1 (Tools)
- Toggle Flashlight: ALT + F (Lights)
- Toggle EFB: TAB (Tools)

- Toggle Drone Lock Mode: 6 (Camera - Drone)
- Toggle Drone Follow Mode: 5 (Camera - Drone)
- Toggle Drone Depth of Field: 3 (Camera - Drone)
- Toggle Drone Auto Focus: 1 (Camera - Drone)
- Toggle Drone Auto Exposure: 2 (Camera - Drone)
- Toggle Drone: SHIFT + X (Camera)
- Toggle Disengage Autopilot: CTRL + 2 (Autopilot)
- Toggle Delegate Control to Copilot: ALT + C (Instruments)
- Toggle Crouch: C (Player Character)
- Toggle Console: ' (Developer Mode)
- Toggle CFD: ALT + 5 (Tools)
- Toggle Avionics Master: CTRL + X (Instruments)
- Toggle AutoRudder: CTRL + P (Flight Control Surfaces)
- Toggle Autopilot Wing Leveler: CTRL + F12 (Autopilot)
- Toggle Autopilot VS Hold: CTRL + F8 (Autopilot)
- Toggle Autopilot Master: CTRL + 1 (Autopilot)
- Toggle Autopilot Mach Hold*: CTRL + F11 (Autopilot)

ADD-ONS AND MODS FOR ENHANCED GAMEPLAY

Microsoft Flight Simulator 2024: Overcoming Challenges and Enhancing Your Experience

Microsoft Flight Simulator 2024 didn't have the most flawless launch. Players reported server overloads, super-long loading times, and missing content that frustrated people. However, this passionately enthusiastic modding community decided to give the experience a makeover. Some of these early problems can be sorted out now with a deluge of add-ons and mods, while you can also unlock new tools and features that enhance the simulation. In fact, such community contributions have been the essential part of raising this game to a whole different level and providing a more polished experience.

Master the Controls: Simplified Keyboard Guides

But some users are finding it daunting to master the complex controls in Microsoft Flight Simulator 2024. Mastering keyboard shortcuts can go a long way in making flying easier.

To help, a detailed guide by redgreen, entitled Default MSFS 2024 All Keyboard Commands, puts every shortcut into easy-to-follow categories that range from camera controls and navigation to engine systems. The guide is formatted as A3, both light and dark theme, in case you want to print it or keep it open on a secondary screen. For those who would refer to a more visual reference, redgreen also has a Keyboard Layout with Default MSFS 2024 Commands. This layout is graphical in nature, mapping out the commands to make learning key functions easier and to streamline your in-flight operations. Whether you are a beginner or an experienced pilot, these tools can help you get the most out of your flying adventures.

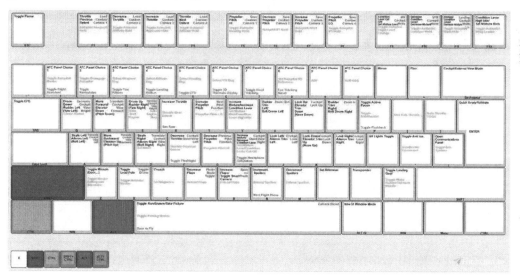

Expand Your View: Custom Camera Views for All Aircraft

The ability to explore the world from different angles inside and outside of the cockpit is among the most exciting aspects of flight simulation. This mod takes it to the next level: Custom Camera Views for All MSFS2024 Airplanes adds customized views inside the cockpit and cabin for each and every standard aircraft in *Microsoft Flight Simulator 2024. Thoughtfully, these views have been assigned to keyboard numbers 0 through 9 for ease of access during your flights.

Setting up the mod is simple: download it, extract the files, and place them in the appropriate folder based on your game installation type. For even more custom perspectives, browse the Custom Views category on Flightsim.to and take your flight experience to the next level.

Smooth Navigation with the Subtle Taxi Ribbon Mod

Subtle Taxi Ribbon is the solution that works for those who depend on taxi ribbons as visual ground navigation aids and can find the default version just too overwhelming. In addition, this mod actually switches out the standard blue ribbon to a more discreet one tinted green, which should hopefully melt seamlessly into the line lights in taxiway centers. The end product, for users, is less destructiveness coupled with effectiveness for great enhancement of realism without robbing it from the general airport ambiance.

Installation is easy: just extract the files to your Community folder and start enjoying a more immersive taxi experience.

Airport Override Checker Resolves Conflicts

There are occasions that come with managing modded and default airports in Microsoft Flight Simulator 2024, where especially in the case of overlapping packages, issues can arise. That's what the Airport Override Checker by leftos is for: it scans your community folder for potential clashes with streamed airport packages and provides easy ways to create overrides using links or empty folders. While links remain the preferred option due to their reliability, both are manageable through the tool's straightforward interface. Though a planned December 2024 update by MSFS will address many of these conflicts, the tool is crucial in between for smooth management of the airports.

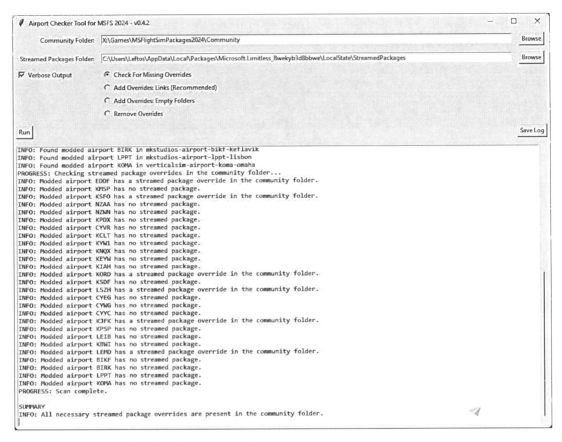

Precision Control with the Sim Rate Selector

Those who want more control of the simulation speed can enjoy a more user-friendly experience using the Sim Rate Selector. This toolbar widget fits neatly into Microsoft Flight Simulator 2024, where one can adjust the simulation speed in real time. If one is slowing down to perform a tricky landing or accelerating to a long flight, this tool gives instant feedback for immediate control.

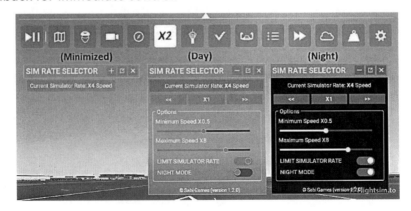

Pre-Flight Planning with the Briefing Panel

Good flight planning is key to a trouble-free mission, and the *Briefing Panel* brings this functionality right into the simulator. This toolbar widget provides easy access to your SimBrief flight plan without leaving the game and proves particularly useful when in VR or on a single monitor. It clearly and concisely displays everything from fuel calculations to routing details, right down to integrating OpenAIP for a real-time map view that will keep you on course from departure to arrival.

Streamlining the Management of Add-Ons Using Addons Linker

In the burgeoning repository of available mods with Microsoft Flight Simulator, navigating can be increasingly tricky to do. It is through this that *MSFS Addons Linker 2020/2024* helps tidy up, activates, and manages your add-ons, both for MSFS 2020 and MSFS 2024, much easier than having to do manually in their default forms. It lets you move your add-ons out of the "Community" folder into a directory of your choice while keeping them working with symbolic links. You can create folders and subfolders for organizing and activate/deactivate groups of add-ons with one click, rename add-ons without destroying their links, and more using this tool. Recent updates include hiding incompatible add-ons, improved preset customization, and display of add-on thumbnails for managing.

Explore More Add-Ons

For a wider range of add-ons and mods, go to flightsim.to/2024, where you'll find a range of content designed for Microsoft Flight Simulator 2024. The site has special sections for specific categories like liveries and sceneries, making it easier to discover enhancements tailored to your needs. You can also filter by base aircraft to view all add-ons available for particular aircraft models. Additionally, later this month, a new feature will be made available allowing you to toggle between MSFS 2020 and MSFS 2024 content while browsing through categories.

CHAPTER 4
AIRCRAFT DEEP DIVE

Experience one of the most exciting careers as a licensed pilot. Imagine yourself flying through the air, traveling to exciting destinations literally anywhere in the world. Wherever your travels take you, the scenery is always spectacular.

Salary Information

The hourly rate of pilots, flight engineers, and flying instructors will depend on experience, aircraft type, and location. Here is a generalized breakdown:

Job Title	Hourly Wage
Air Pilot	$22.85 - $77.88

Salaries would vary depending on experience, length of service, flight hours, category of aircraft, and geographic location. Base salaries may be augmented by several fringe benefits, bonuses, per diems, and other pay awards.

Air Canada

The salary expectations for a narrowbody Captain at Air Canada can reach an average of $215,000-$290,000 per year, plus expenses. Captains go on to fly widebody after 11-15 years, earning $315,000-$350,000, plus expenses. Air Canada has very generous benefits, including a pension and Annual Incentive Plan.

Air Canada offers some of the highest salaries in Canada, but for the first four years, pilots earn a fixed rate regardless of the aircraft they fly. The airline guarantees a minimum of 75 flying hours per month for salary calculations. New pilots can expect to earn around $57,375 in their first year, with senior Captains who work overtime earning over $400,000.

Porter Airlines

On average, Porter pilots make $119,322 per year; the highest-paid go up to $265,000. Porter is offering a signing bonus for Direct Entry Dash 8 pilots from $15,000 - $25,000 depending on experience. Porter will hire more than 1,200 new pilots over the next four years and offers the fastest upgrade to a narrow-body jet Captain in Canada.

Labor Market Outlook

The demand for air pilots in Canada has rebounded quickly post-pandemic and is expected to outstrip the number of candidates available. This trend is likely to continue over the forecast period of 2022-2031, leading to a national pilot shortage. In Ontario, the job prospects for pilots are excellent between 2023 and 2025 due to increased global air travel, routes, and the expansion of low-cost carriers, thus creating opportunities in the long run in the industry.

GENERAL AVIATION AIRCRAFT OVERVIEW

What is General Aviation (GA)?

General Aviation (GA) is the term given by the International Civil Aviation Organization (ICAO) for all civil aviation operations other than scheduled air services and non-scheduled air transport operations for hire or remuneration. Sometimes it is referred to as General Aviation/Aerial Work because this category includes aerial work.

What does GA include?

General Aviation and Aerial Work entail a whole number of activities which include:

- Recreational flying (balloon, glider, and sport aircraft)
- Pilot training
- Business aviation
- Agricultural services (such as crop spraying)
- Emergency medical services (such as the transport of critically ill patients, human organs, and medical supplies)
- Airborne traffic monitoring
- Civil search and rescue operations
- Law enforcement and firefighting
- Aerial survey work
- Aerial photography
- News gathering
- Sightseeing and air tours
- Flight demonstrations

These activities account for about 40 million flight hours annually, with recreational flying making up roughly a quarter of that. The global GA sector involves around 350,000 aircraft and 700,000 pilots, according to IAOPA Europe.

GA in the United States

The U.S. has the largest aviation market globally, with about 65% of GA flights used for business and public services. Over 90 percent of the 220,000 civil aircraft in the U.S. are GA aircraft; and more than 80 percent of the 609,000 U.S. pilots are certified to fly GA aircraft. The most significant segment of GA is business aviation. According to the National Business Aviation Association (NBAA), the use of GA aircraft for business boosts the United States economy by $150 billion annually.

Safety of GA

Like commercial aviation, some of the leading causes of fatal accidents in GA are loss of control in flight and controlled flight into terrain (CFIT). Other common causes include system/component failures, mid-air collisions, and unintended flight into Instrument Meteorological Conditions (IMC).

In the U.S., the GA fatal accident rate in 2021 was 0.95 per 100,000 flight hours, while the overall accident rate was 5.26 per 100,000 flight hours. For comparison, the international scheduled airline fatal accident rate in 2019 was much lower, at 0.17 fatal accidents per million flight hours, according to the International Air Transport Association (IATA).

COMMERCIAL AIRLINERS: COCKPITS AND FEATURES

Welcome to the fascinating world of aviation, where the cockpit is considered the nerve center of every aircraft. This guide will walk you through the cockpit, the space where pilots control every aspect of the plane's journey, from takeoff to landing. As you go further, you'll realize that the cockpit is much more than just a seat for the pilot and co-pilot and an array of instruments.

What's in a Name? Cockpits, Flight Decks, and Crew Stations

Quite a lot of aviation terms originate from nautical language, and "cockpit" is not an exception. During the initial stages of flying, pilots flew in a cramped, open-air structure of wood and fabric, akin to a "cockpit" on a small sailing boat from where a coxswain does the steering. For this reason, originally, the term was used. Fast forward to today, and modern aircraft boast sleek flight decks with touchscreens, plush sheepskin seats, and advanced controls; hence the term "flight deck" has become common. For a more technical description of the area, the term of choice for many engineers is "crew station".

Which term you use depends on your audience. For military and general aviation or those with traditional aviation knowledge, "cockpit" is still widely used. In commercial aviation, such as for airlines and cargo operators, "flight deck" is the preferred term. Engineers, when designing the space, will likely use "crew station," but for now, we'll stick with the simpler term "cockpit" as we take a look at some real-world examples, starting with the Cessna 172.

All the parts of traditional Cessna 172 Cockpit

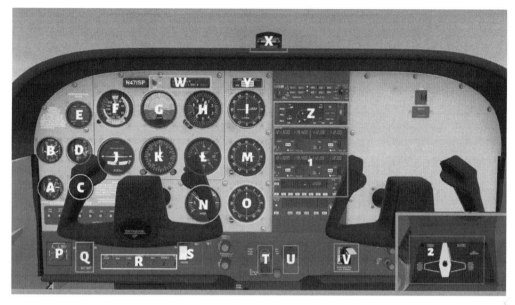

Here's an overview of the cockpit instruments and their functions with the corresponding alphabet letters:

A - Engine Oil Indicators: Shows the pressure and temperature of the engine oil.

B - Fuel Quantity: Indicates how much fuel is on board.

C - Vacuum Gauge / Ammeter: Displays the vacuum pump pressure that powers the attitude and heading indicator.

D - Fuel Flow: Shows the fuel consumption rate in gallons per hour.

E - Digital Clock: Displays the current Zulu time (SIM).

F - Airspeed Indicator: Provides the current airspeed of the aircraft.

G- Attitude Indicator: Displays the aircraft's orientation relative to the horizon.

H - Altimeter: Shows the aircraft's altitude above mean sea level (MSL).

I - VOR Receiver with Glideslope: Displays the glideslope and localizer needles for ILS approaches.

J - Turn Coordinator: Indicates the aircraft's roll movement.

K - Directional Gyro: Shows the direction the aircraft is heading.

L - Vertical Speed Indicator: Displays the rate of climb or descent in feet per minute.

M - VOR Receiver: Measures the bearing to the selected VOR station.

N - Tachometer: Displays the engine's revolutions per minute (RPM).

O - ADF Bearing Indicator: Points towards the selected heading from the NAV system.

P - Ignition Switch: Starts the engine by providing a spark to the fuel/air mixture.

Q - Master Switch: Turns the aircraft's electrical system on or off.

R - Electrical Switches: Controls the exterior lighting and fuel pump.

S - Avionics Master Switch: Powers the avionics bus.

T - Throttle: Controls engine power.

U - Mixture: Regulates the amount of fuel injected into the engine.

V - Flap Switch: Shows the current flap position and adjusts the flap angle.

W - Annunciator Panel: Displays warning lights about the engine's status and includes a test/brightness switch.

X - Autopilot Source: Displays the currently selected autopilot mode.

Y - Standby Compass: Shows the aircraft's current heading.

Z - GPS (Garmin GNX375): Displays a map with flight details.

1 - Com Radio / Transponder: Shows the currently tuned ATC frequency.

2 - Fuel Tank Selector: Allows the pilot to select which fuel tank(s) to draw from.

IN A NUTSHELL: KNOWING THE COCKPIT

The cockpit is the heart of every aircraft, whether it be a large airliner, like Boeing, or a general aviation plane. It houses very specialized parts and systems put to different uses for safe and effective flying. The basic components in the cockpit would include the flight controls, instrument panel, navigation systems, and control surfaces. The tradition with yokes and pedals to digital in modern cockpits of aircraft, such as the ones that Airbus jets use, all play a crucial role in the form of aircraft operation.

The Principal Components of a Cockpit and Their Functions

At the center of every cockpit are the flight control systems. The yoke-a side-stick in some aircraft, such as Airbus-allows the pilot to control the plane's roll and pitch, while the rudder pedals control yaw. Real-time information such as speed, altitude, and engine performance are provided through the instrument panel, with digital displays now offering far more precise data. In addition, control surfaces such as ailerons, flaps, and rudders assist in controlling the movement of the plane in the air.

From Pedals to Yokes: Controls of the Pilot

The yoke and rudder pedals make for the basic flight control. The yoke determines the roll and pitch of the plane, while the rudder pedal adjusts the yaw. Most contemporary cockpits use computerized fly-by-wire technology, which manipulates these motions with much more precision, so that the aircraft would be easier to handle.

Instrument Panel: Important Information within Reach

There's a lot of equipment within that instrument panel to display important in-flight information to the pilot. Whereas older cockpits utilized analog gauges in depicting speed and altitude, new cockpits, known as glass cockpits, represent information on advanced displays-the PFD, or Primary Flight Display, and ND, Navigation Display-that provide comprehensive real-time information relevant to flight.

The Evolution of Cockpit Design: From Traditional to Glass Cockpits

Cockpit design has undergone a number of significant changes over the years. The early cockpits utilized independent instruments, while the modern ones often boast integrated glass displays, thereby reducing pilot workload and increasing safety. These electronic flight instruments minimize the amount of information and make it easier for pilots to manage the aircraft systems and navigate effectively.

What is the Yoke and Pedal's Role in the Cockpit?

The yoke and pedals are used to control the aircraft's movement. Together, they enable the pilot to control the speed, altitude, and direction of the plane for smooth flight operations.

DETERMINING THE ROLE OF THE YOKE IN AIRCRAFT CONTROL

The yoke is a crucial tool in the cockpit, enabling the pilot to control the aircraft's pitch (up and down movement) and roll (side-to-side movement). It is a primary control for adjusting the aircraft's attitude.

How Pilots Utilize the Rudder Pedals for Navigation

In addition to the yoke, rudder pedals help pilots manage yaw—the aircraft's rotation around its vertical axis. By using these pedals, pilots can steer the plane, especially during turns and while taxing on the ground.

How to Combine Yoke and Pedal Controls

Mastering the combination of yoke and pedal movements is essential for smooth flight operations. By perfectly coordinating these controls, pilots ensure efficient takeoffs, landings, and maneuvers, even in challenging conditions.

Understanding the Function of Flight Controls for Takeoff and Landing

During takeoff and landing, pilots rely on a range of controls, from throttles to flaps, to ensure smooth and safe operations. Proper use of these tools is crucial for aircraft of all sizes.

Controlling the Aircraft: From Large Airliners to Smaller Aircraft

While the basic principles of flight control remain the same, flying larger airliners is more complicated because of the additional systems and controls in the cockpit. The larger the aircraft, the more complex and diverse the systems in its cockpit.

How Does the Instrument Panel Assist Pilots?

It contains keys to critical flight data: altitude readings, airspeed, and how the engine is performing. It also contains systems for controlling functions such as landing gear and flaps, depending on the specifications of the aircraft.

Decoding the Flight Deck: Differences in Various Aircraft Types

Each type of aircraft has its own design of the flight deck. While all flight decks incorporate displays intended to help pilots, the complexity of these displays and number of systems increase with the size of the aircraft.

Interpreting the Gauges and Indicators for Safe Flight

The gauges and indicators act like vital signs of the aircraft, showing altitude, airspeed, and fuel, among other things. These systems enable pilots to monitor the status of the aircraft and ensure a safe flight.

The Importance of an Electronic Flight Instrument System

The introduction of EFIS has completely revamped cockpit design. In glass cockpits, the EFIS permits pilots to access vital data through displays such as the PFD and ND, which makes flight management easier and more accurate.

Flight Management and Air Traffic Control: Keeping Track from the Cockpit

Modern FMS and communication with ATC are very important in managing the aircraft's flight path. These systems enable the pilot to navigate through busy airspace, monitor weather conditions, and maintain contact with ground control.

How Display Systems Enable the Pilot to Control the Flight

It involves the varied display systems that show in real-time both internal and external conditions of the flight to inform the pilots and enable them to make decisions on controlling flights.

UNIQUE COMPONENTS OF A PROPELLER PLANE COCKPIT

The Propeller's Role in Aircraft Operation

The propeller is the centerpiece in a propeller plane that produces the forward motion required for flying. The pilot can vary the speed and pitch of the propeller by use of the control system to change the motion of the aircraft through the air.

The Trailing Edge and Control Surfaces

The key control surfaces, such as the ailerons and flaps, are on the trailing edge of the wing, at the back of the airplane. Both of these devices help control the aerodynamics of the plane. Ailerons, which provide roll control, are located toward the tip of the wing whereas flaps are found farther toward the body of the wing and closer to the centerline of the aircraft. Lift is increased during slower speeds by the use of flaps and greatly aid during takeoff and landing.

Ailerons are the primary means of controlling the roll of all fixed-wing aircraft; propeller aircraft, in particular. These control surfaces enable the pilot to guide the aircraft, especially when making turns. Ailerons are only one part of a coordinated control system that also includes the elevator and rudder.

Flaps and Ailerons: Operation during Takeoff and Landing

Flaps are high-lift devices that enable the aircraft to obtain greater lift at low speeds, essential during takeoffs and landings. However, flaps also increase drag and hence are not efficient at higher speeds. Therefore, during cruising, the flaps are retracted. Ailerons, along with the flaps, play an important role in ensuring smooth and controlled takeoffs and landings.

The Control System in Propeller Aircraft

Propeller aircraft have a complicated control system with several interconnected components: throttle control, which regulates the speed of the air; propeller control, which adjusts the thrust; and gear control, which operates the landing gear. Each component helps to maintain the speed, altitude, and overall performance of the aircraft.

Specifics of the Flight Deck in Propeller Aircraft

In addition to this, a propeller-driven aircraft flight deck would typically have an added number of specialized gauges, including the propeller RPM indicator. The latter displays the propellers in revolutions per minute, as opposed to jet aircraft using the N1 and N2 indicators showing the RPM of the jet engines. These types of gauges will help the pilot monitor the performance of the aircraft's propulsion system.

Iconic Aircraft in MSFS 2024

F-16 Fighting Falcon (United States)

The F-16 Fighting Falcon, also known as the F-16, is a multirole single-engine jet fighter originally designed by General Dynamics, now Lockheed Martin, for the United States and more than a dozen other countries. Initially conceived in 1972 for a lightweight, cost-effective air-to-air day fighter, the F-16 has evolved into an all-weather multirole aircraft and is considered one of the most successful fighter platforms ever built. The first delivery to the US Air Force took place in 1978.

Measuring 49 feet in length and with a wingspan of 31 feet, the F-16 is powered by a turbofan engine that generates 23,000 to 29,000 pounds of thrust, enabling speeds greater than Mach 2. It's equipped with a 20mm rotary cannon and can carry a range of bombs and missiles on under-wing and fuselage attachments. With a typical combat load, the F-16 weighs around 23,000 pounds. It derived fame for its effectiveness in air-to-air and ground-attack missions in such conflicts as the 1982 Israeli-Syrian War and the 1990-91 Persian Gulf War. The F-16 is still the most in-demand fighter and is flown by over 20 nations around the world.

MiG-21 Fighter (Soviet Union)

The MiG-21 is a lightweight, single-engine interceptor from the Soviet Union, first flown in 1955. With an operating speed more than twice that of sound, it was initially a simple, low-cost day fighter. Its design placed great emphasis on maneuverability, ease of maintenance, and the ability to operate from less-developed airstrips. More than 9,000 MiG-21s were produced in 32 different versions for Soviet and over 40 foreign air forces, including a Chinese-licensed version. It served as the primary high-altitude interceptor for North Vietnam and remained the backbone of Arab air forces throughout the 1970s.

Tupolev Tu-95 Bomber (Soviet Union/Russia)

The Tupolev Tu-95, which first took to the skies in 1954, is a turboprop bomber that turned out to be one of the longest-serving aircraft within the Soviet and later the Russian strategic arsenal. This device, with its long and distinguished career, was called the "Bear" for the mission of carrying cruise missiles, having been in continuous use over the decades, with Russia continuing to keep more than 50 operational to this day. The initial conversion from jet-propelled, piston-engine designs to a turboprop revealed an incredibly resilient and robustly dependable bomber.

Bf 109 Fighter (Germany) The Bf 109, commonly known as the Me 109, was Nazi Germany's most important fighter aircraft in World War II. Designed by Willy Messerschmitt, the Bf 109 first entered service in 1937 and fought in the Spanish Civil War, where it easily outclassed Soviet fighters. The Bf 109 was equipped with various machine guns and, later in the war, received a much more powerful fuel-injected engine and automatic cannons. During the early years of World War II, it was the major fighter for Germany, especially during the Battle of Britain. At low to medium altitudes, the Bf 109 proved to be exceptional, but at higher altitudes, it was no match for the British Spitfire. Nonetheless, it remained a formidable opponent in the skies until the end of the war.

CHAPTER 5
NAVIGATING THE WORLD

This image highlights the system requirements for Microsoft Flight Simulator 2024 with a sleek and modern computer setup. It features key hardware components such as a powerful processor, high-performance graphics card, plenty of RAM, and fast storage. The setup is enhanced with flight simulation accessories like a flight yoke, throttle quadrant, rudder pedals, and multiple monitors displaying realistic flight data from the game. The icons representing hardware specifications in the professional background design point to the fact that a robust system is key to an immersive and seamless flying simulation experience.

How to Use Microsoft Flight Simulator 2024:

Step 1: Become Orientated with MSFS 2024

- To start with, launch the simulator and create a new pilot profile or load an existing one.
- Familiarize yourself with the interface, including the Primary Flight Display (PFD), Multi-Function Display (MFD), and Navigation Display.

- Browse through the menus for aircraft selection, weather and time changes, and adjustment of simulation preferences.

Step 2: Choose Your Aircraft

- Select an aircraft suitable for your needs in terms of performance, range, and handling.
- Take some time to familiarize yourself with the onboard systems such as autopilot, navigation, and communication systems.

Step 3: Filing Route and Destination

- Use the navigation tools to set your route:
- **Flight Plans:** Load predefined routes or create your own.
- **Nearest Airports**: Pick an airport and let the simulator generate a path.
- **Free Flight:** Fly anywhere without a set destination.

Step 4: Use Autopilot for Assistance

- Stabilize the plane's altitude and speed before activating autopilot.
- Hit the AP (Autopilot) button on the cockpit interface.

Adjust your settings:

- Use the ALT wheel to set your desired altitude.
- Press to choose your climb mode: VS (Vertical Speed) or FLC (Flight Level Change).
- Set the switch to NAV mode to follow your route.
- Click HDG (Heading) button. Manual adjustment may be done here.

Step 5: Monitoring and adjustments in flight

- Monitor altitude, speed, and heading.
- Change the autopilot settings if your course or altitude needs correction.
- Use the navigation tools to track progress and revise your flight plan as needed.

Step 6: Explore and Enjoy the Skies

- Soak in the detailed landscapes and realistic flight dynamics.
- Try different weather and time of day, and configuration of aircraft.

- Advanced navigation techniques such as GPS approaches or VOR navigation.

Additional Tips for an Enhanced Experience

- Employ inbuilt tutorials to learn vital skills, such as instrument flying or handling emergencies.
- Test different aircraft and scenarios to broaden your expertise.
- Join online communities to connect with fellow enthusiasts, share insights, and pick up valuable tips.

Enjoy your journey into the skies with MSFS 2024! 🛫

REAL-WORLD MAPS AND FLIGHT PATHS

Since the release of the first Microsoft Flight Simulator in 1982, flight simulators have made many people excited. Yet as the technology and graphics improve vastly, the core of every flight simulator remains the same-to create a hyper-realistic experience for flyers, from a total amateur to an experienced pilot.

But are these virtual tools just for fun, or can they genuinely aid in flight training? Let's break it down.

What Are Flight Simulators?

Flight simulators are more than just games—they're immersive programs designed to replicate real-world flying. Whether you're a curious beginner or a professional pilot, these simulators offer something for everyone.

Here's what makes them stand out:

Variety of Aircraft to Fly: From a small Cessna to jumbo Airbuses; many simulators also include rotorcraft, seaplanes, historical aircraft, and sometimes very special challenges, such as landing the space shuttle.

Global Explorer: With highly detailed sceneries and 3D-rendered landmarks, you can virtually fly to every place on Earth and enjoy realistic landscapes.

Specialized Features: Some add-ons allow you to fly inside a military jet or do crazy stunts in coordination with airshows.

Why Use Flight Simulators?

Flying a real airplane is expensive, but with a simulator (priced at around US$60), you can take to the virtual skies at any time. Here's why they're valuable:

1. Accessible and Affordable: Practice landings, try advanced maneuvers, or just enjoy flying exotic aircraft without the real-world expense.

2. Realism for Training: Modern simulators recreate cockpits and avionics with stunning accuracy, allowing you to practice emergency procedures, instrument approaches, and more.

3. Learning at Your Own Pace: Simulators allow you to slow things down, helping you master procedures and think ahead during complex scenarios.

4. Community and Fun: Join online networks, engage with virtual air traffic controllers, or team up with friends for formation flying or competitive dogfights.

Do Flight Simulators Enhance Flight Training?

For the student pilot, simulators can indeed be useful but are hardly a panacea. They really shine as a study aid by allowing one to visualize procedures and gain familiarity with the conceptual elements of aviation; however, some things simply do not translate well into real flying.

Excellent Learning Tool: The simulator is basically a high-tech way of doing "chair flying," which is a method in aviation whereby pilots practice procedures step by step to develop muscle memory and flow. Unlike using the imagination or static cockpit posters, simulators offer interactive, responsive digital cockpits for a more immersive experience.

Training Limitations: While flight simulators help in refining your skills, the real-life feel of the controls or aircraft dynamics is not captured. Similarly, the regulatory frameworks, like Part 141, would also limit how much time one spends on the simulator, which would be credited towards actual flight training.

Summary

These flight simulators are an excellent tool for both aviation enthusiasts and pilots alike. They combine the thrill of flying with practical learning opportunities, offering a cost-effective way to hone skills and explore aviation. While they can't fully replace real-world training, simulators remain an invaluable resource in building knowledge, confidence, and precision in the skies. Whether one flies for fun or to support their aviation journey, flight simulators open up a world of possibilities.

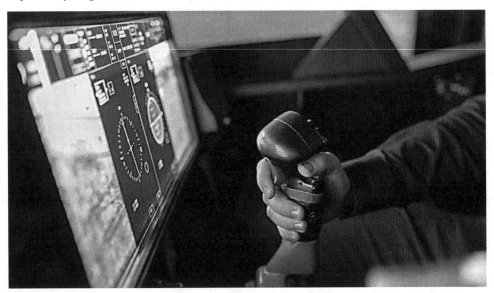

Advantages of Training with a Flight Simulator

Flight simulators possess more advantages compared to disadvantages, thus being truly useful in the training of pilots.

1. Building Habits and Familiarity: Flying the plane is about developing routines, going by checklists, and familiarity with the cockpit. Simulators excel in replicating cockpit layouts to help pilots practice efficient workflows, so-called "cockpit flows," instinctively knowing what to do and where to look.

2. Mastering Flight Rhythms: Simulators are very realistic in the replication of the behaviors of certain aircraft. That enables the pilots to practice important features of flying, like the length of a downwind leg, how an airplane behaves when flaps are extended, or power adjustments for just the right glideslope on landing.

3. Refreshing Skills: For pilots who haven't flown in a while, simulators are great for getting the rust off. They can refresh their muscle memory and techniques at no cost before returning to the air with an instructor.

4. Transitioning Between Cockpit Types: Simulators are excellent for getting used to new cockpit layouts, such as transitioning from traditional steam gauges to a glass cockpit or vice versa.

5. Training for Emergencies Safely: Simulators permit pilots to practice safely those situations that are too dangerous in the real world. For example, they can simulate an engine failure at low altitude or practice cloud breakout-important skills that enhance safety without actually risking lives or equipment.

Disadvantages of Flight Simulator Training

While flight simulators are advantageous, there are some limitations, and actual flying is still indispensable.

1. Possible Bad Habits: The students could be accustomed to habits such as overemphasizing the instruments, inadequate outside scanning for traffic, and other crucial items in actual flight like incorrect rudder usage.

2. Limited Situational Awareness: In a simulator, it feels unnatural to look around; this makes developing the habit of scanning for traffic challenging. This may make students less prepared when facing real airspace challenges. VR technology has helped, but it is far from being solved.

3. Limitation of Physical Interaction: The use of a mouse or touchscreen to manipulate switches and controls in the simulator can be very different from using them in an actual cockpit. Muscle memories developed on the simulator won't directly translate into use on the plane.

4. Not Real-Life Feeling: In simulators, it's not possible to reproduce the actual feeling of flying-aerodynamic forces during stall, steep turn, and landing. Kinesthetic feedback during the execution of these maneuvers is an important point for pilots to be well acquainted with and can be achieved only during flight.

5. Awkward Interface for Certain Activities: Simple tasks like changing radio frequencies or turning on a landing light can feel cumbersome in a simulator compared to the seamless actions in a real cockpit.

Conclusion

Flight simulators are very good tools for knowledge building, procedure practice, and preparation for critical situations. However, they can't fully replicate the real-world experience of flying. Combining simulator practice with actual flight time ensures pilots develop both technical skills and the physical instincts needed for safe and effective flying.

Using Flight Simulators for Instrument Training

Flight simulators are especially useful for those pilots building their instrument rating. Although simulators have some limitations in private pilot training, most of these concerns become less relevant when it comes to instrument flying.

1. Mastering Core Skills: Simulators are ideal to master the key instrument skills such as VOR tracking, DME arcs, holds, and various types of approaches. These procedures work in the simulator just as they do in a real plane.

2. Realistic Approach Practice: You have access to downloadable approach plates from around the world. With the realistic approaches, all the instruments and frequencies function just as they would during an actual flight, giving you the best possible training environment.

3. Procedure-Oriented: Instrument flying is more about procedures, checklists, and habits than simply following instruments. For example, flying an ILS approach isn't just about following the "crosshairs" to the runway; it's also about setting up the approach correctly, briefing it, and being prepared with a missed approach procedure. Simulators are great for practicing these steps in detail.

4. Guided Training: The most effective use of a simulator is during an appropriate training phase and under the guidance of your flight instructor. Practice setting up and briefing approaches, flying them to minimums, executing missed approaches, and entering holds-just as you would in real-world instrument training.

5. Failure Management: Simulators are in a league of their own when it comes to practicing instrument failures in complete safety. You could practice flying on the backup instruments during a vacuum failure or navigating through icing conditions. With realistic checklists and procedures, you can practice declaring an emergency without any risk.

USING THE WORLD MAP INTERFACE

A new flight simulator often means adapting to a new user interface, but thankfully, Microsoft Flight Simulator 2024 is quite close in design to its predecessor. If you're used to MSFS 2020, you'll find much of the UI to be quite similar, which should make the transition smoother.

That said, one of the more obvious updates is within the main menu, which is perhaps the most changed of any element from the 2020 version. Let's dive in and explore what's new and improved!

The home menu in Microsoft Flight Simulator 2024 now puts a strong emphasis on the world view while introducing a refreshed interface. The new game modes take center stage, but don't worry-classic features like the activities menu and free flight options are still easy to find.

First of all, up in the top-right corner, is a new profile section: with your username, quick links to settings, notifications, and the in-sim Marketplace, and a messaging feature, all put together and easily accessible, selecting your username opens your pilot profile.

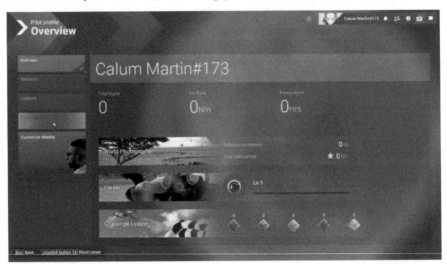

You will be able to look over and analyze your career progress and ranking in the challenge league, among other important statistics found in your virtual log as a pilot.

For the activity's menu, they also keep the same horizontal scrolling and options: flight training, rally races, challenges for low altitude, etc.

The free flight section is largely unchanged from MSFS 2020 but has been cleaned up, making it much more organized than before.

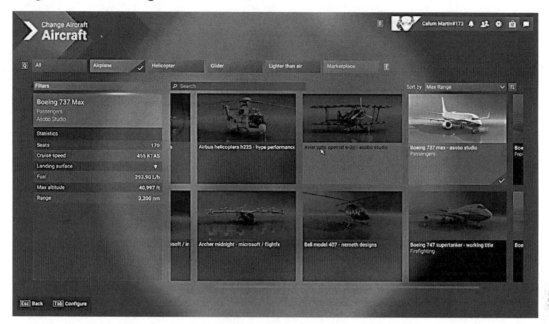

When selecting an aircraft, you can scroll the list, search, sort, or filter to find what you need quickly. A nice new feature is the ability to filter planes purchased through in-sim Marketplace. Clicking "configure" opens configuration options for livery, weight, balance, and other familiar settings.

The free flight menu still offers its main functionality as it did in the previous iteration, allowing you to fiddle with flight conditions: You can set weather and time to live, use a preset, or create your own. You'll also be able to manage air traffic and multiplayer sessions. Perhaps one of the biggest new features is setting weather or air traffic to real conditions from within the last 24 hours, something developers have been teasing for some time now.

Navigating the world map works just as it did before. Major airports are marked with icons, while smaller airfields, helipads, and other points of interest become more prominent as you zoom in.

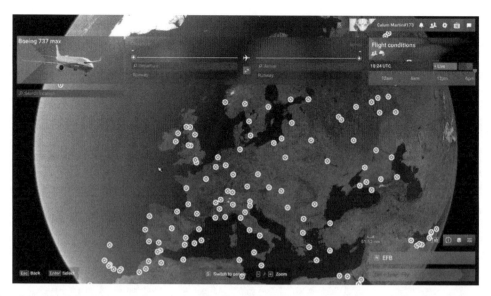

Back in the aircraft selection screen, the 'Configure' allows access to explore a lot of options. Here you are allowed to change liveries and variants of an aircraft, show its statistics, alter the payload among many others. Also, at free flight mode, on the walk-around mode, many details including engine covers and chocks can be edited.

One of the most interesting new features in Microsoft Flight Simulator 2024 is the universal EFB, which was developed by Working Title. This tool works in every aircraft and offers necessary flight information, such as procedures, flight numbers, payload, and more, directly within your cockpit.

Once you have finished selecting a flight, clicking 'Fly' smoothly transitions you to the simulation world, seamlessly zooming into the map for your starting location.

Inside the sim, the toolbar is still similar but the colors are updated and the design modernized to match the sleek UI style of the main menu.

In career modes, the interface includes special features such as a career progress tree and the ability to monitor missions taking place all over the world, further deepening the experience.

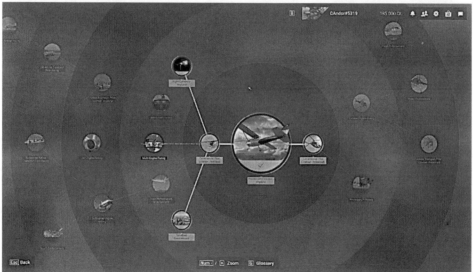

The user interface and menu system in Microsoft Flight Simulator 2024 are for the most part identical to those in the 2020 version. It does feel cleaner, though, more polished, and more refined. The updated loading screen adds a much smoother and faster feel to the overall experience.

CHAPTER 6
ADVANCED PILOTING TECHNIQUES

Using AI Control as an Autopilot in Flight Simulator

If you want an easy way to make a plane fly itself in Flight Simulator, you can employ an AI Control, an autopilot of sorts. Here's how you enable it:

1. First of all, open the top-of-the-screen toolbar.

   - On Xbox, press the left stick to bring it up.

2. Select the AI Control option.

In the AI Control menu, you'll find three settings:

   - **Checklist Assist:** Helps with pre-flight and in-flight procedures.
   - **Manage Radio Comms**: Automates radio communication.
   - **Control Aircraft**: Enables the autopilot, passing control to your AI co-pilot.

Select Control Aircraft to enable the autopilot and allow the AI to fly the aircraft.

This feature, when turned on, enables you to continue with your original flight plan. It's quite useful if you get lost or cannot handle the aircraft in bad weather.

In addition to the simplified autopilot available through AI Control, Microsoft Flight Simulator offers a variety of keyboard shortcuts for managing the in-aircraft autopilot system-if the plane supports it. These hotkeys will give you direct access to a variety of autopilot functions for greater control.

Here's a list of default autopilot shortcuts:

- Autopilot On: `ALT + Z`
- Autopilot Off: `SHIFT + ALT + Z`
- Airspeed Hold: `ALT + R`
- Decrease Reference Altitude: `CTRL + PGDOWN`
- Increase Reference Altitude: `CTRL + PGUP`
- Toggle Approach Hold: `CTRL + A`
- Toggle Attitude Hold: `CTRL + T`
- Toggle Localizer Hold: `CTRL + O`
- Toggle Mach Hold: `CTRL + M`
- Toggle Master Autopilot: `Z`
- N1 Hold: `CTRL + S`
- Decrease N1 Reference: `CTRL + END`
- Increase N1 Reference: `CTRL + HOME`
- NAV1 Hold: `CTRL + N`
- Decrease Reference Airspeed: `SHIFT + CTRL + DEL`
- Increase Reference Airspeed: `SHIFT + CTRL + INSERT`
- Decrease Vertical Speed Reference: `CTRL + END`
- Increase Vertical Speed Reference: `CTRL + HOME`
- Toggle Wind Levelers: `CTRL + V`

These commands allow for finer control, enabling easier aircraft handling during complex flight situations.

A quick reminder: AI Control and autopilot usage in Flight Simulator isn't always perfect, as the feature is known to sometimes falter, according to launch notes on Steam: "Autopilot may struggle with altitude and speed targets," and in practice AI Control sometimes overlooks speed warnings.

For example, taking off from Monument Valley airport with AI Control enabled saw the system unable to safely clear the surrounding mountains. While AI Control is still a useful tool, it's good to remember these foibles until such time as future updates remedy them.

Mastering Takeoffs, Landings, and Crosswind Challenges

Microsoft Flight Simulator 2024 Review: A New Era of Virtual Aviation

It's taken some time, but Microsoft Flight Simulator 2024 has finally leveled out into smooth skies. The initial launch was rough, with server overloads making the game unplayable for the first 24 hours and bugs appearing in the days that followed. But after 58 hours spent navigating its numerous refinements, building a career, capturing breathtaking views of iconic landmarks, and, yes, flying for free, I can say with confidence, "They've done it again." A rocky start paved the way for this installment to impressively build off of its predecessor, offering a new and polished experience.

Visual Enhancements and Realism

One of the most striking upgrades in Flight Simulator 2024 is its improved graphics, especially when it comes to seasons and weather. Based in Maine, I often explore familiar terrain in the simulator. The attention to detail is astounding—whether it's late-autumn leafless trees, the contrast of evergreen pines, or the vibrant hues of Vermont in October, the seasonal changes are beautifully accurate. You can even regulate the depth of snow, and observe realistic tracks left from planes taxiing through snow, mud, or tall grass.

The game also features special events, such as the April 2024 solar eclipse. By changing date and time, you get to relive the grim lighting and gradual darkness that this celestial event caused-from 35,000 feet aloft.

Lighting has improved dramatically, especially within the cockpit. The shadows fall more naturally now, every knob and button have a realistic shade, and scratches on windows react dynamically to sunlight, sometimes even obscuring your view. These small touches really raise the level of realism.

Performance and Hardware Demands

While the visuals are great, they do not come cheap. My Radeon RX 7900XT GPU was sweating, reaching up to 99% usage in places where the ground detail was denser. In-flight, it hovered around 80%. This is especially evident in the new feature that enables players to land, get out of their aircraft, and explore on foot. Hopefully, Asobo Studio will do some optimization in the performance with future updates, making this feature less heavy on hardware.

Career Mode: A Structured Path to the Skies

Career Mode is the crowning addition to Flight Simulator 2024, giving structured missions and goals to players. Starting with a home airport selection, you work toward a Private Pilot License. This is largely the same training from the 2020 release, but serves as a good refresher. For seasoned pilots, you can skip ahead directly to the exam.

In your career, earning credits and progressing require completing jobs, which will become increasingly complex as the level of certification rises. For instance, with a PPL, you start with short sightseeing flights. Later, with a Commercial Pilot License, you unlock much more lucrative missions: aircraft deliveries, search-and-rescue operations, and much more. The career system is structured like a skill tree, with certifications unlocking new opportunities. There's even a parallel tree for helicopter pilots, offering a similar progression tailored to rotorcraft.

A Nod to the Past

Flight Simulator 2020 set the bar for blending real-world mapping data with unsurpassed simulation. Its effortless ability to let players take to the skies anywhere on Earth was a revelation. Flight Simulator 2024 builds upon that tradition, refining it with a smoother interface, smoother transitions, and new gameplay elements.

Final Thoughts

Despite the rocky launch, Microsoft Flight Simulator 2024 proved itself a worthy successor. Enhanced visuals, refined lighting, and new career opportunities seal its place as one of the best. While performance optimizations are sorely needed, particularly in ground-level exploration, it's an awing way to explore our planet. From aviation enthusiasts to casual gamers, Flight Simulator 2024 takes virtual flying to new heights.

UNDERSTANDING CROSSWIND OPERATIONS

Crosswind conditions can be a real challenge for pilots during takeoff and landing, demanding skill and precision to ensure safe operations. Whether you're an experienced pilot or still learning, mastering crosswind techniques is key to staying proficient and confident in tough weather. In this article, we'll go over the basics of handling crosswinds, important safety tips, and special considerations for airports with obstacles.

Crosswind takeoffs and landings are performed when the wind does not blow directly down the runway. In such conditions, the wind exerts a sideward force on the aircraft, which may cause the airplane to be blown off course. For such situations, a pilot should possess specific techniques to overcome these forces and maintain control during the most critical phases of flight.

Key Techniques for Crosswind Takeoffs

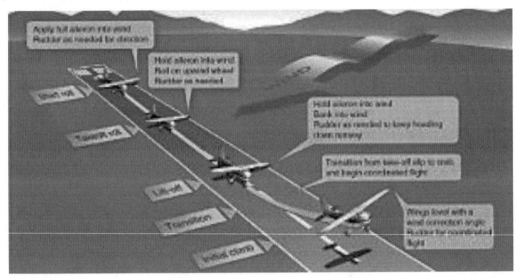

1. Aircraft Alignment: The nose of the aircraft should be aligned directly into the wind during takeoff to minimize crosswind effects.

2. Rudder Control: Coordinated rudder inputs are applied to maintain alignment with the runway centerline and to prevent the aircraft from veering off course.

3. Control Inputs: Ailerons are applied to prevent the upwind wing from lifting too early to ensure proper wing alignment.

4. Gradual Application of Power: The power should be gradually increased in order to avoid the aircraft being blown off track by the crosswind.

Crucial Habits of Crosswind Landings

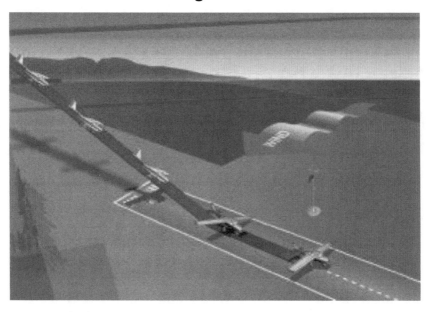

1. Crabbing: Approach the runway with a slight crab angle to account for the crosswind, keeping the plane aligned with the centerline.

2. Side Slip: Before landing, perform a controlled side slip to align the aircraft with the runway and minimize drift.

3. Touchdown Technique: Touch down with the upwind wheel first to allow the aircraft to naturally straighten as weight shifts to the downwind wheel.

4. Maintain Control: Continue applying rudder inputs during the rollout to counteract any remaining crosswind forces.

Safety Considerations at Airports with Obstacles

When flying in crosswind conditions, a pilot must be very much aware of runway length, surface conditions, and other possible obstacles. Other factors, such as terrain or buildings near an airport, can further complicate crosswind operations.

Safe Operations at Airports with Obstacles

1. Performance Calculations: Consider the aircraft's performance limitations considering runway length, elevation, and temperature.

2. Obstacle Clearance: Know the obstacles in relation to the runway and plan your departure and arrival accordingly.

3. Wind Shear Awareness: Be aware of wind shear effects, especially in proximity to terrain features, which can affect aircraft handling and performance.

4. Go-Around Decision: Always be prepared to go around if conditions deteriorate or obstacles pose a safety risk.

Conclusion

Crosswind takeoffs and landings are an essential accomplishment for every pilot, ensuring safety and proficiency in various weather conditions. By understanding the principles of crosswind flight and applying the right techniques, pilots can confidently handle challenging conditions. Remember, safety should always be the priority, especially when flying at airports with obstacles. Careful planning and execution are key to reducing risks and maintaining safe operations.

IFR VS. VFR FLYING

Before you even take off in an aircraft, you will encounter two very important acronyms, VFR and IFR, significant in how flights are navigated. These stand for Visual Flight Rules and Instrument Flight Rules, respectively, referring to two different sets of flying regulations. Which one a pilot flies depends on many factors, including their certification as a pilot, the weather, the class of airspace the flight is in, and the purposes of the flight. Let's break down exactly what each of these means in aviation.

VFR vs. IFR: What's the Difference?

VFR (Visual Flight Rules) and IFR (Instrument Flight Rules) are two different systems that guide pilots in navigation. VFR allows pilots to navigate by sight, which is great to have in good weather conditions. On the other hand, IFR relies on instruments to guide the aircraft, hence becoming vital whenever visibility is poor-for example, when there is fog, rain, or night flying.

How VFR Flying Works

When flying under VFR, pilots rely on visual references to navigate-such as rivers or cities-pilotage skills, and sometimes GPS technology. It is similar to taking a road trip in a car where the pilot can determine their route and altitude within certain airspace boundaries. Unlike IFR flights, VFR pilots are not required to maintain constant communication with air traffic control or adhere to a strict flight plan. This gives them more freedom, although controlled airspaces may require additional coordination.

This flexibility also means VFR pilots can enjoy activities like sightseeing or just flying leisurely in clear skies.

VFR Limitations

Even as VFR affords so much freedom, there are some important rules to keep in mind. First and foremost, VFR flight is only possible in conditions of Visual Meteorological Conditions (VMC), meaning the weather should be good enough for decent visibility with the aircraft clear of clouds to allow a pilot to navigate visually without relying on instruments. Minimum visibility and cloud clearance criteria for VFR flights have been specified separately.

ALTITUDE BAND	AIRSPACE CLASS	MINIMUM FLIGHT VISIBILITY	MINIMUM DISTANCE FROM CLOUDS
At and above 3050m or 10000ft AMSL	A,B,C,D,E,F,G	8 km	1500 m horizontally 300m or 1000ft vertically
Below 3050m or 10000ft AMSL and above, 900m or 3000ft AMSL or, 300m or 1000ft above terrain, whichever is the higher	A,B,C,D,E,F,G	5 km	1500 m horizontally 300m or 1000ft vertically
At or below 900m or 3000ft AMSL or, 300m or 1000ft above terrain, whichever is the higher	A,B,C,D,E	5 km	1500 m horizontally 300m or 1000ft vertically
At or below 900m or 3000ft AMSL or, 300m or 1000ft above terrain, whichever is the higher	F,G	5 km (*)	Clear of cloud and with the surface in sight

VFR MINIMA TABLE — BAA TRAINING

STAYING SAFE WITH VFR FLYING

When flying under VFR, it's important to stick to the rules of visual flight. If you're tempted to fly through a cloud, keep in mind that another pilot might be heading in the opposite direction.

There are several responsibilities VFR pilots need to keep in mind, including:

- Maintaining visual contact with other aircraft
- Being aware of and avoiding wake turbulence

Forecasting possible weather changes

The VFR pilot must be prepared and alert for any change that may occur while navigating their aircraft in this mode; that way, flying will always be smooth and safe.

Procedure to Fly IFR

IFR means flying by instruments when the visibility is poor, and you cannot rely on external references. This is necessary in such conditions as fog, rain, or night flying. You can legally fly IFR in clear conditions, too, known as VMC, but it's primarily used for IMC: poor-weather flying.

Unlike VFR, IFR allows flights in more restrictive airspaces, such as Class A, which requires more stringent controls.

To fly under IFR, pilots must have radio capable of two-way voice communications and the navigation equipment necessary to complete their route. This more often than not includes ground-based aids such as VOR or GPS. Instruments required for IFR include a gyroscopic rate-of-turn indicator; a slip-skid indicator; a sensitive altimeter which adjusts with barometric pressure; a clock with hour, minute, and second hands; and attitude indicator to keep the airplane properly aligned.

Filing an IFR Flight Plan

To fly under IFR, pilots must possess an Instrument Rating and file a detailed IFR flight plan in advance. It contains all the details of the flight, including route and waypoints, and coordination with air traffic control. Most pilots will use electronic systems approved by aviation authorities to file their IFR flight plans, which ensures smooth communication with ATC.

Once the flight plan is filed, the next step is to request clearance from ATC using standard communication protocols. It's important to stay alert to changing weather conditions, as sudden shifts from clear skies to storms can occur unexpectedly.

Commercial Pilots and IFR

For commercial pilots, IFR is essential during most of their flight, especially when en route. It ensures safety and consistency regardless of the weather. Probably, the most tragic single example in connection with the relevance of sticking to IFR procedures involves the crash of Turkish Airlines Flight 452. It crashed near Isparta, on September 19, 1976, en-route from Istanbul to Antalya, killing all 154 people aboard. After investigations, it came up that the crew was on a VFR flight. The First Officer mistakenly identified the dark area as the Mediterranean Sea, which was the Taurus Mountains, and the highway lights as runway lights heading to Antalya Airport. This incident highlights the importance of following IFR for safety.

Why Pilots Choose IFR or VFR

Whether to fly a flight under VFR or IFR depends on several factors including the pilot rating, the weather condition, and the nature of the flight.

Many pilots prefer IFR, especially in conditions of low visibility or at night, because it ensures continuous communication with air traffic control. This is particularly helpful in busy, complex airspaces, such as those around major European cities like London, Paris, or Frankfurt, where it streamlines navigation and addresses the need for multiple clearances. IFR allows instrument-rated pilots to navigate more efficiently through crowded airspaces and restricted zones.

On the other hand, some pilots prefer VFR because it offers more freedom. They can choose their own flight path and altitude, which is especially appealing for leisure flights. VFR flights also don't require as much equipment, making them more cost-effective, particularly for small aircraft. Flying under VFR also demands more from the pilot in terms of situational awareness and spatial orientation, which can improve overall piloting skills.

From VFR to IFR Training

IFR flying requires additional training for pilots beyond that required for VFR flying. This means gaining an Instrument Rating, which allows them to fly the aircraft with instruments rather than by looking out of the windows. The training focuses on instrument flying and prepares pilots to operate under IFR conditions. This rating is especially useful for those pilots who would like to fly in any weather conditions and not be grounded by bad visibility. It's also a necessary step for those who want to fly commercial aircraft in the future.

In Summary

Mastery of both VFR and IFR is very important for a pilot. Basically, VFR depends upon the visual references, while IFR depends upon the instruments and coordination with air traffic control to move through bad weather conditions. A pilot should be aware of both sets of rules for safety and efficiency in shared airspace. In this way, pilots can make informed decisions about situations and navigate safely and effectively.

Frequently Asked Questions on VFR And IFR

What is the difference between IFR and VFR?

The fundamental difference is that VFR is based on visual navigation, while IFR basically uses instruments for navigation in conditions of low visibility.

Which is harder: IFR or VFR?

IFR is generally regarded as more challenging because pilots have to rely on their instruments and manage more complex procedures, especially in poor weather. However, pilots with an IFR rating are also trained to handle both VFR and IFR scenarios.

Do airline pilots always fly IFR?

Yes, airline pilots typically fly under IFR because doing so assures safety and adherence to regulations, especially in controlled airspace.

Do private jets fly IFR or VFR?

Private jets can fly both IFR and VFR, depending on the weather, regulations, and qualifications of the pilot.

What are the limitations of VFR flying?

The limitations to VFR flying include maintaining the terrain and other aircraft in sight, observing airspace restrictions, visibility and cloud clearance, and being able to navigate safely.

EMERGENCY PROCEDURES AND FAILURES

Microsoft Flight Simulator 2024 has made a huge leap in simulating engine failures, making the game more realistic and immersive than ever. The game now includes a variety of engine failure scenarios, from complete engine loss to partial malfunctions, which require players to use their skills and knowledge to handle the situation in real-time. This raises the stakes of every flight, making it feel more authentic. Key features include:

- **Dynamic failure modes:** The engine can fail for various reasons, from wear and tear to decisions made during flight.
- **Innovative response protocols:** For safety reasons, pilots need to act fast while maintaining control of the aircraft.
- **Training simulations:** New tutorials will better prepare players for possible failures and teach them that anything can happen in aviation.

The simulator's technical depth goes into the details of engine operation, allowing players to see how their actions affect the aircraft's performance. Each malfunction challenges the pilot's decision-making abilities and understanding of aerodynamics, providing a hands-on learning experience. Advanced graphics and realistic sound effects enhance the realism of these failures, making each emergency feel urgent and life-like. For players, mastering both controls and problem-solving in the air become a new, game-changing feature for veterans in flight simulators.

- **Realistic soundscapes**: Audio of engine failures is planned to raise the sense of urgency during emergencies.
- **Integrated weather factors:** Environmental conditions can deteriorate because of engine failures and thus create another layer of challenge.
- **Community feedback system:** Players can submit suggestions in order to improve failure mechanics to keep the experience fresh and engaging.

Understanding the Influence of Emergency Procedures on Gamers

Emergency procedures for Microsoft Flight Simulator 2024 are designed to perfectly capture the intense pressure felt by pilots during real crises. When an engine fails, players are thrown into desperate situations that require immediate, life-or-death decisions. It applies a very intricate algorithm to make the consequences appear realistic, and every choice gives a completely different outcome. The player will have to stay calm under pressure by handling quick-time events that would test their knowledge about the aircraft systems and emergency procedures. This will definitely help increase player engagement, with an added benefit of greater understanding of aviation principles.

That drastically affects gameplay, as it completely changes the feel of flying. The pilots have to rely on checklists for systematic responses, such as managing engine failure, looking into altitude, and preparing emergency landings. Every flight is a lesson in how to handle a crisis, while at the same time honing valuable skills such as situational awareness and resource management. These scenarios often provide feedback that influences future gameplay, in turn reinforcing learning and adaptation. With its emphasis on emergency procedures, Microsoft Flight Simulator 2024 allows even the most routine flights to become learning journeys, revealing valuable insights into pilot competencies and the intricacies of flight dynamics.

The Importance of Emergency Training

Training for emergencies is crucial. Many flight schools emphasize the importance of practicing these situations, as the FAA is increasingly testing new pilots on their ability to handle such emergencies. But it's not just about passing tests—real accidents do happen, and being prepared is key.

As a home flight simulator owner, you should include failure scenarios and adverse weather conditions in around 20% of your training sessions. It may feel uncomfortable to step out of your comfort zone, but emergency training is the best way to learn how to handle high-risk situations.

You can practice a variety of emergencies in a flight simulator, including aborted takeoffs, engine failures after takeoff, spin recovery, icing, lost communications, low fuel, and more.

VFR Emergency Scenarios for Simulation

Pilots—both students and professionals—use flight simulators to improve their skills in various VFR or Visual Flight Rules scenarios. It's a fun way to stay motivated and enhance your flying techniques. Here are some VFR emergencies you can simulate:

Scenario Set Up - Stuck in Cloud Layer on VFR

You have become stuck in a cloud layer while on a VFR flight and should start communicating with ATC declare an emergency, and instruct you down through the cloud. A high-pressure interaction to practice for a challenging real-life emergency.

Hot High Altitude

Set the temperature to 35ºC (95ºF) and depart from a high-altitude runway. This is particularly challenging for pilots who have not flown in high-altitude conditions before, as the high-density altitude greatly affects aircraft performance. Practice makes perfect in this scenario.

Pop-up Thunderstorms en-route to a Coastal Destination

This scenario combines a bunch of challenges, from unexpected weather changes to handling with ATC. It is perfect for improving your overall decision-making and adaptability.

Nighttime Alternator Failure

Try this first over an airport with minimal lighting and services, then try it over a well-equipped one. In either case, the challenge will be there for sure in navigating and dealing with electrical failures in low visibility.

Complete Instrument Failure (Except the Compass)

With the dependence on GPS systems in today's world, flying a compass alone may seem highly antiquated, but it's a great way to perfect your basic navigation skills. It can be challenging but rewarding, and it refines your ability to rely on conventional flight instruments.

Low Oil Pressure Over a Busy City

Low Oil Pressure Engine Failure over Congested Metropolitan Area While flying in a congested metropolitan area, an engine failure forces critical decisions to be made swiftly to ensure the safety of all on board.

Engine Failure After Takeoff

This is one of the most valuable training exercises to practice. Depending on your altitude, you have options, and it takes some speed to manage. You can also try several variables such as wind, obstacles, or a different runway to see how each of them affects your response.

Pitot-Static Problem During Climb

The pitot-static system is vital to your flight's instrumentation. Adding night and a climb to a simulated pitot-static failure really complicates things and will challenge your instrument flying skills.

This set of scenarios will go a long way in better preparing you for an actual emergency and building confidence in your ability to handle one when it occurs.

Technical Insights: Mechanical Failure Simulation in Microsoft Flight Simulator 2024

Microsoft Flight Simulator 2024 has brought realism to the next level, especially regarding mechanical failure simulation. Advanced algorithms and physics-based systems are used in order to create detailed representations of all kinds of engine malfunctioning that pilot can potentially face in real life. These allow the user to go through different challenging scenarios, putting one's piloting skills to test under pressure.

Some of the key failure types being introduced include:

- **Power Loss**: A sudden loss in engine power, rendering flight controls nonresponsive.
- **Overheating**: Engine overheating problems that the player has to work around with emergency procedures.
- **Fuel Starvation**: Scenarios of fuel mismanagement impacting performance.
- **Mechanical Breakdowns**: Unexpected failures which require quick thinking and decision-making.

In fact, its attention to detail for the mechanical failure simulation is further than it being for more immersive reasons. It is a practical training tool for both future pilots and aviation enthusiasts. It encourages users to think critically, applying knowledge of aerodynamics and aircraft systems to troubleshoot and resolve issues, thus enhancing their learning experience. Besides, one is allowed to adjust the frequency and severity of the failures, which means the game can suit any user, from a complete beginner to a seasoned expert.

Suggestions to Improve the Experience of Engine Emergencies

To further enhance the engine emergency experience in Microsoft Flight Simulator 2024, it would be great if there were more features that make the process even more challenging for the developers. First of all, detailed failure modes specific to various aircraft engines would allow expansion of the range of possible scenarios. This may be supported by random component failures, variations related to altitude or weather conditions, and more complex responses, which require quick decisions by the pilots.

Further, adding dynamic environmental factors like wind direction, turbulence, and temperature effects during engine failures could increase the stakes and make the players fly accordingly in real time.

Enhanced training modules on engine emergencies would similarly help new and experienced pilots. The use of interactive simulations that realistically model real-life protocols of engine failure would help the players learn how to apply effective emergency procedures, boosting both confidence and skill. A multiplayer mode where players can cooperate in emergency drills can encourage community engagement, whereby pilots can share strategies and experiences. Finally, a realistic feedback system could be implemented in which, after managing engine failures, the pilots receive a detailed review of their performance, fostering continuous improvement and deepening the understanding of aviation safety principles.

CHAPTER 7
EXPLORING GLOBAL DESTINATIONS

The older I get, the more I find myself reflecting on the places I've lived and traveled, in awe of the growing list of countries I still want to see, such as Japan. I feel increasingly grateful for the many places I've had the chance to experience, and Microsoft Flight Simulator 2024 has become a fantastic way to relive those memories.

With its remarkable photogrammetry and advanced digital elevation maps, the "digital twin" of Earth in this simulator is a visual wonder to behold. These realistic details enable me to fly over my old neighborhoods, revisit national parks, or retrace some of the memorable coastlines I haven't seen in years. I can even step out of the aircraft and explore nearly any location around the globe, and you can too.

Flying Through Memories

In a recent interview with Xbox Wire, Jorg Neumann, the Head of Microsoft Flight Simulator, said, "What I realized during the development of Microsoft Flight Simulator (2020) is that the most emotional stories are the ones which already reside in us. Earth may just be a rock, a hill, or a tree, but it holds special meaning for different people because of their memories. These are very personal stories. It's almost a universal platform for an emotional connection because we all live here, and this is what our planet looks like."

I watched the sunrise from the top of Haleakalā decades ago.

Neumann echoes a sentiment I too have felt since spending my time with Microsoft Flight Simulator 2024. Indeed, it is a great simulator, replete with several aircraft and modes such as Career and World Photographer, but what struck a chord with me was the emotional feel of flying over familiar places in that much detail.

He tells the story of when he said, "During the pandemic, I missed my parents a lot. My dad is in his mid-90s, and I was scared I wouldn't see him again, everything being so uncertain, so I flew to their house in Microsoft Flight Simulator (2020), landed by the lake, and called them - 'I can't be there with you in person, but I'm as close as I can get because I'm looking at our house.'"

Neuschwanstein Castle is often recognized as the inspiration for Disney's Cinderella Castle.

With Microsoft Flight Simulator 2024, it feels so much closer to reality. It is emotionally impactful because now the trees around the lake are accurate, the ground and water look just as they should. It is incredible how all those memories come rushing back: the feeling of jumping into the lake as a kid, playing with friends, swimming for the first time. Now you can digitally recreate everything you once experienced.

Revisiting Favorite Places

I similarly felt a rush of emotions revisiting some of my own favorite places. Memories I hadn't thought about in years bubbled to the surface, such as watching the sunrise at Haleakalā crater on Maui, walking across San Francisco's Golden Gate Bridge, wandering the streets of Paris, or getting lost in Venice. Flying through these familiar spots in Microsoft Flight Simulator 2024 brought all those feelings back.

These were personal favorites of Neumann's first stops in the simulator, too. "The first place I went to was Kauai," he told me. "Then, I visited Grindelwald, where I used to go skiing. I also took a walk around the Alps and checked out New Zealand-a place I love. After that, I took a look at around 10 places I've been in real life and how accurately they were mapped out and then went on a movie tour to view locations from 'Indiana Jones', 'Lord of the Rings' and 'Out of Africa.

San Francisco will always have a piece of my heart.

The latest updates have taken it to a whole new level for the entire community by making flight simulation more realistic than ever. Environments are vastly more detailed, with great terrain, rock, and even water conditions that make for not just more functional and immersive experiences but also vastly more authentic ones. Not only are these environments as real as possible, from the right type of leaves on the trees to precise rocks on the ground.

FAMOUS AIRPORTS AND CITIES

Microsoft Flight Simulator 2024 is not far away now, and from what we have seen so far, it promises spectacular visuals of the world we will fly through. As most flights start and finish at airports, Asobo hasn't left us wanting. While every Earth airport will have an auto-generated version, the new simulator will feature up to 160 "upgraded" airports, depending on the edition you choose. In this article, we'll go over all the confirmed airports, each handcrafted by Asobo or their network of developer partners, that you can look forward to in the upcoming release.

Seattle Tacoma International Airport (KSEA – shown here in MSFS 2020) will be in MSFS 2024

Confirmed New and Upgraded Airports in Microsoft Flight Simulator 2024

All upgraded airports from Microsoft Flight Simulator, the release of 2020, will be included but with improvements to elevate them to a higher threshold. They are not just the same airports from the previous edition; they have been improved upon for MSFS 2024. To this date, two new airports have been confirmed for MSFS 2024:

- KGCN – Grand Canyon National Park (USA)
- LEBB– Bilbao (Spain)

Apart from these, a total of 155 airports which were part of MSFS 2020 (including both the base edition and post-launch updates) will be carried over into MSFS 2024. These will be spread across various editions of the game.

MSFS 2024 Standard Edition Airports List

North America:

- KASE – Aspen / Pitkin County (USA)
- KTEX– Telluride Regional (USA)
- KJFK – John F. Kennedy International (USA)
- KLAX – Los Angeles (USA)
- KEB– Nanwalek (USA)
- KMCO– Orlando (USA)
- KSEA– Seattle-Tacoma (USA)
- KSEZ – Sedona (USA)

- CYTZ – Billy Bishop Toronto City (Canada)
- CZST– Stewart (Canada)

Europe:
- LXGB – Gibraltar (Gibraltar/UK)
- EIDL– Donegal (Ireland)
- LFLJ– Courchevel Altiport (France)
- LFPG– Paris Charles de Gaulle (France)
- LOWI– Innsbruck (Austria)
- LPMA– Cristiano Ronaldo Madeira Int (Portugal)

Australia & Oceania:
- YSSY – Sydney (Australia)
- NZQN– Queenstown (New Zealand)
- CAMA– Bugalaga Airstrip (Indonesia)

Asia:
- RJTT– Haneda (Japan)
- VQPR – Paro International (Bhutan)
- VNLK – Tenzing-Hillary (Nepal)

South America:
- SGBL – Rio de Janeiro (Brazil)
- SPGL – Chagual (Peru)
- SEQM – Mariscal Sucre International (Ecuador)

Caribbean & Central America:
- TNCS – Juancho E. Yrausquin (Dutch Saba)
- TFFJ – Gustaf III Airport (France / Saint Barthélemy)
- MRSN– Sirena Aerodrome (Costa Rica)
- MHTG – Toncontin International (Honduras)

Africa:
- HUEN – Entebbe International (Uganda)

That is only 30, but the company has been working for the last four years with its developer community to add many more through free World Updates, and with MSFS 2024's new streaming technology, these will be easily accessible. It brings the number of airports featured in the Standard Edition up to 150. Further details on these will be released shortly.

MSFS 2024 Deluxe and Premium Deluxe Airports Highlighted

Deluxe Edition

The Deluxe Edition of Microsoft Flight Simulator 2024 adds five more upgraded airports from MSFS 2020, bringing the airport count in this edition to 155. The various airports span iconic destinations to further your flight experiences globally:

- LEMD – Madrid–Barajas (Spain)
- EHAM – Amsterdam Schiphol (Netherlands)
- HECA – Cairo (Egypt)
- FACT– Cape Town (South Africa)
- KORD – O'Hare International (USA)

Premium Deluxe Edition

For the ultimate experience, the Premium Deluxe Edition adds five more major airports, totaling 160. These are some of the busiest airports in the world and include long-haul aircraft operations that would be perfect to fly in upgraded planes such as Boeing 787-10 and Boeing 747 "Dreamlifter". The Premium Deluxe airports are:

KDEN– Denver (USA)

- KSFO – San Francisco (USA)
- OMDB– Dubai (UAE)
- EDDF – Frankfurt (Germany)
- EGLL – London Heathrow (UK)

From short hops down the road to intercontinental flights, these extended updates bring varied destinations in remarkable detail.

HIDDEN GEMS, LESSER-KNOWN LOCATIONS

Long-haul flights will take hours, and this is where autopilot becomes most important in Microsoft Flight Simulator 2024. At this moment, MSFS 2024 does not have an easy click-it-and-forget-it option where the AI will take control. Instead, you manually set all the settings, adjust everything, just as you would on a real flight, before you actually engage autopilot. If you're having a hard time with this, the following guide will walk you through the basics, making your next long-haul or carrier flight smoother and more manageable.

How to Turn On Autopilot

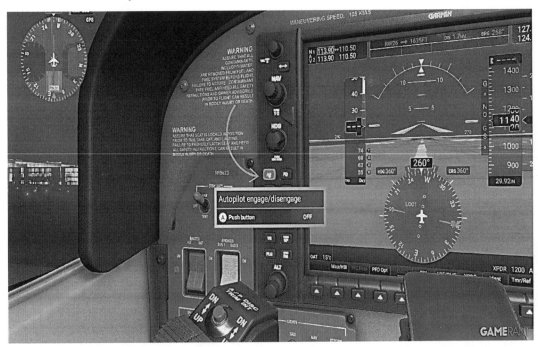

Autopilot Basics Explained in Simple Terms

1. Take Off and Stabilize: First, take off and make sure your altitude and speed are stabilized.

2. Engage Autopilot (AP): Find the AP button, which is usually located around the primary flight display, and click it to turn on the autopilot.

3. Set Altitude: Choose your desired altitude with the ALT wheel, usually located near the AP button.

4. Select Climb Mode: Select one of two climb modes:

- VS (Vertical Speed): Selects your rate of climb in feet per minute.
- FLC (Flight Level Change): Climbs or descends while holding a selected speed.

5. Select Navigation Mode:

NAV Mode: Follows your GPS flight plan automatically.

HDG Mode: Allows directly setting flight direction with a HDG wheel.

Most of the aircraft featured in Microsoft Flight Simulator 2024 come equipped with these modes, and are thus very easy to set and manage for flying on autopilot. In fact, it can be as simple as enabling the system to climb and descend and following the already set flight plan or heading provided by you.

Autopilot Basics

Understanding Autopilot: The Basics

While the exact setup and buttons might be different from one aircraft to another, the core principles of autopilot-Heading, Navigation, and Altitude-remain the same.

Here's how they work:

Heading Mode (HDG)

In heading mode, the autopilot will maintain aircraft heading without needing direct input of the wheel. Rotate the **HDG wheel** on your display to set or adjust the heading, and the autopilot does the rest. This mode is really useful when you do not have a flight plan, yet still want to have some control over the heading of the airplane, but the autopilot does the rest regarding altitude or speed.

Navigation Mode (NAV)

Navigation mode enables autopilot to follow a GPS flight plan automatically correcting course as necessary to keep on route. If not currently on a flight plan, hitting the "Nearest" button on the PFD provides quick input of a GPS direct course heading toward an airport of proximity.

Altitude Management (ALT)

Altitude mode maintains the aircraft at a set elevation. Use the ALT wheel to choose your desired altitude. For autopilot to adjust altitude, however you must also select a climb or descent mode:

Vertical Speed Mode (VS): Regulates the altitude by adjusting the rate of climb or descent. This is set via the Nose Up or Nose Down buttons.

Flight Level Change Mode (FLC): Adjusts altitude based on airspeed. Set your desired speed in knots, and the autopilot will manage the climb or descent using throttle power.

By mastering these basic modes, you'll have full control over the autopilot and can ensure a smooth flight, whether you're following a flight plan or managing settings manually.

CHAPTER 8
MULTIPLAYER AND COMMUNITY FEATURES

A Decade of Innovation in Gaming

Microsoft Flight Simulator has redefined gaming over the past decade, a real showpiece for what is possible in simulation games. With the entire world at your fingertips, you might wonder how developers could surpass the last installment. Let's dive in to explore what's new, including the highly anticipated multiplayer feature.

Is Microsoft Flight Simulator 2024 Multiplayer?

Yes, Microsoft Flight Simulator 2024 does have multiplayer, and even better, it's cross-platform.

Whether you're playing on Xbox or PC, you can connect with friends on either platform. Note that the game does not include split-screen functionality. For shared play, you'll either need multiple devices or to share the screen with someone at home.

Release Date

Mark your calendars as Microsoft Flight Simulator 2024 launches on November 19, 2024.

This latest version promises a lot more for aviation enthusiasts, continuing to push the limits of realism and immersion. Everyone from casual gamers to flight sim enthusiasts is making serious investments in high-end gaming setups to elevate their experience even further.

Is It on Xbox Game Pass?

Yes, Microsoft Flight Simulator 2024 will be coming to Xbox Game Pass.

Given that it is a Microsoft title, one would expect nothing less than its inclusion on Game Pass. Though optimized for high-performance PCs, it will also run-on Xbox Series S and X. The unfortunate thing, though, is that players on either PlayStation or Nintendo Switch won't get to see this game.

Gameplay Enhancements

Prepare for a visual treat and outstanding gameplay, along with its new features in Microsoft Flight Simulator 2024.

Not only does this pack a punch in the visual sense, but it also opens doors to new adventures such as:

- Medevac Missions
- Cargo Operations
- Firefighting Challenges

With an expanded lineup of aircraft and the ability to travel virtually anywhere, this installment offers something for every aviation enthusiast. Whether you're a seasoned pilot or a curious beginner, the skies are yours to explore.

JOINING THE MSFS COMMUNITY

The Community Folder is where you will add third-party content such as new aircraft or scenery to enhance your MSFS experience. However, how you find this folder depends on how you installed the game. Here's a quick guide to help you locate it with ease.

Best Method (Works on All Systems)

1. Start MSFS and do the following:

- Options → General Options. Once opened, look for the Developers tab and click where it says Developer Mode and slide it to <On> At this moment, an additional bar above all others should appear; then from that newly appeared toolbar locate Tools → Virtual File System.

Expand the section Packages Folders, click on Open Community Folder.

2. Tips and Variations: You may want to make a shortcut to the folder on your desktop so that opening it again can be easy in the future. You may quit the developer mode with Dev Mode → Exit Dev Mode at the menu top.

If you install an add-on, restart MSFS to ensure the new content loads properly.

Alternative Method: Use Windows Explorer

Prefer to navigate yourself? Here's how:

1. Enable Hidden Files in Windows Explorer - this is required to be able to see the AppData folder.

2. Follow the path, depending on how you installed MSFS:

Microsoft Store Installation

C:\Users\USERNAME\AppData\Local\Packages\Microsoft.FlightSimulator_RANDOM\LocalCache\Packages/community

Steam Installation:

C:\Users\USERNAME\AppData\Roaming\Microsoft Flight Simulator\Packages\Community

Replace "USERNAME" with your Windows username.

With these methods, you should be able to find the Community Folder easily and enjoy customizing your simulator!

How to Find and Move Your Community Folder in MSFS 2024

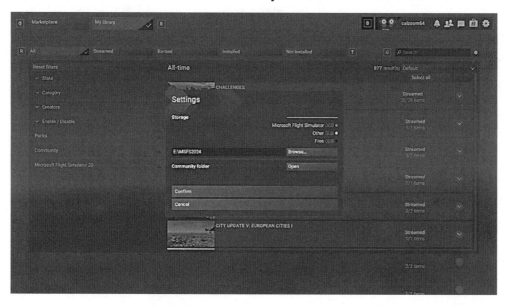

The Community Folder in Microsoft Flight Simulator 2024 is a central location for third-party add-ons management. Unlike MSFS 2020, the installation process for MSFS 2024 doesn't allow you to pre-select the location during setup. This article will help you find your Community Folder and show you how to change its location if needed.

Where is the MSFS 2024 Community Folder?

In MSFS 2024, the Community Folder is located in a default path within your system's local directories. The typical path would be something like this:

C:\Users\[USERNAME]\AppData\Local\Packages\Microsoft.Limitless_8wekyb3d8bbwe\LocalCache\Packages

Replace [USERNAME] with your Windows username.

Quick Access Tips

Use File Explorer: Open Windows File Explorer and, in the address bar at the top, type %LOCALAPPDATA%. This is a shortcut that will take you directly to the Local folder where the Community Folder is located.

Show Hidden Folders:

  If you can't see the AppData folder, you need to enable hidden folders in your settings in File Explorer.

Changing the Location of the Community Folder

While the guide focuses on finding the folder, you can move it using a symbolic link (symlink). This allows you to move the folder to any other drive that you may find more convenient while the simulator works fine.

1. Move the Community Folder to your desired location.

2. Open a Command Prompt as an administrator.

3. Use this command to create a symlink:

mklink /D "Original Folder Path" "New Folder Path"

Replace Original Folder Path and New Folder Path with your folder paths.

With this, you can manage your add-ons in a more streamlined way and save storage without hurting your simulator.

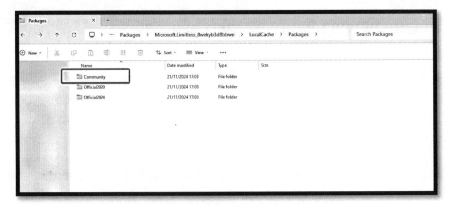

The Community Folder is a bit cumbersome to find in MSFS 2024; you could create a shortcut, but that is not a very good solution. Sometimes it will cause problems with long file paths, and if you like to store your add-ons on another drive for ease of organization or storage management reasons, then changing where the folder is located is going to be a better solution for you.

REAL-TIME MULTIPLAYER FLIGHTS

Last August, Microsoft introduced the newest version of its seminal Flight Simulator, extending the franchise's remarkable 38-year legacy and cementing its place as Microsoft's longest-running product line. Coming via the publisher Xbox Game Studios, this latest iteration takes realism to new heights. Gamers can now expect to see environments in exquisite detail, life-like aircraft textures, advanced lighting, and flight characteristics that are more realistic than ever. From the details in the Boeing 787 Dreamliner to the Cessna 172 and Beechcraft B350, the detailed renderings of all 20 aircraft included, along with individual airports, are nothing short of stunning.

Cockpits are so meticulously designed that nearly every switch is functional. Real-time features take immersion to the next level—air traffic and weather are faithfully replicated. For example, if Denver International Airport is experiencing snow and 40 planes are in its airspace according to FlightAware, you'll navigate your approach through a virtual snowstorm alongside those 40 aircraft, mirroring reality.

The view of Earth from above is one of aviation's greatest thrills, and Flight Simulator masterfully recreates the entire planet in high resolution, from pole to pole. Real-time star constellations, moon phases-even atmospheric effects like twinkling stars, engine exhaust distortion, and sun "notching" when rising or setting-are all part of the experience.

Users have extensive control over their virtual flights, adjusting everything from flight control sensitivity to the state of the weather, time of day, and their view of the aircraft and surroundings.

The effort brought in loads of data from different fields such as aerodynamics, geodesy, photogrammetry, and optics. Fronting this development was video game company Asobo Studio from Bordeaux, France, working along with global partners including Bing Maps, which provided geospatial data; Meteoblue, for providing the details about the atmosphere; Blackshark.ai, for machine learning purposes; and FlightAware to track real-time air traffic data globally.

I was uniquely privileged to serve on this ambitious project as a contractor-researching airplanes and airports that would help set the base for Microsoft's dream of creating this masterpiece.

Microsoft tapped into Bing Maps and other advanced services to beautifully capture the vibrant essence of the Pacific islands. And what better way to see such amazing scenery than from the comfort of a Piper Cub on a leisurely flight?

Soaring with Precision

For that hyper-realism in Flight Simulator, Asobo Studio has taken high-resolution scans of real aircraft using the Artec Leo 3D scanner, capturing details as fine as half a millimeter. And gamers get to see those planes in incredible detail, from scuff marks on windows to tiny nicks on levers.

It wasn't just visuals-the team also recorded the full range of sounds inside and outside the aircraft, including the echoes of rain or snow hitting the cockpit. As for flight dynamics, they studied how air interacts with 1,306 individual surfaces of each airplane to create an authentic control system.

According to Asobo Studio's founder and CEO, Sebastian Wloch, every aircraft was reviewed by advanced pilots or test pilots to make sure it handled precisely. That means when virtual pilots fly an A320, it handles exactly as the real aircraft would-offering the closest experience possible to actually flying one.

There are plenty of third-party accessories like yokes, throttles, and joysticks that let players move beyond the traditional mouse and keyboard for a more immersive experience.

Bringing the World to Life

The team at Asobo merged high-resolution satellite imagery with aerial photography and highly detailed photogrammetric data from Bing Maps to recreate the planet in remarkable detail. This enormous dataset, which continues to grow, has swelled to three petabytes and counting. Although most of the imagery is taken from directly overhead, some is captured at an angle, all in 2D.

Turning such flat data into a smooth, uninterrupted 3D world was going to require some magic; Asobo teamed up with Blackshark.ai-an Austrian company specializing in machine learning. Blackshark's team of 50 experts created advanced algorithms harnessed to the power of Microsoft Azure's cloud computing. Initially guided by human input, these systems learned to render and color Earth's features, from accurately depicting the height of 1.5 trillion trees to erasing shadows created by clouds when necessary, and colors true to life.

The result is a stunning digital Earth at three feet resolution for the entire planet; three-to-ten-inch resolution for 300,000 square miles of dense urban area, and 58,000 square miles of city area in such fine detail that you almost can walk down the streets virtually.

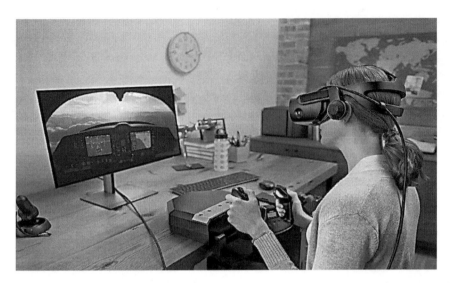

To take the Flight Simulator experience to the next level, players can dive into the action with a virtual reality headset, making the simulation feel incredibly lifelike.

Flying Conditions Made Real

What's a flight simulator without the sky? Thanks to Meteoblue, a Swiss pioneer in weather modeling, the atmosphere in Flight Simulator is divided into 250 million detailed compartments, extending from ground level up into the stratosphere. These store data of temperature, wind speed, humidity, pressure, rain, snow, and other weather elements. "We use this data to recreate the sky and its conditions in real time," says Meteoblue cofounder Mathias D. Müller. Using both historical and live data from the ground stations and satellites, the system reproduces weather patterns with incredible fidelity, even modeling molecular interactions to show how weather interacts with aircraft, from icing on wings to rain streaking across windshields.

In the case of air traffic, the simulator taps into real-time data from FlightAware, which updates its servers second by second with the actual positions of aircraft in the sky. That means virtual pilots experience real-world conditions, from the glow of a sunset-lit thunderstorm to other aircraft approaching airports, mirroring reality down to the second. Players can even choose to see other Flight Simulator users' planes flying nearby.

Atop of that, each scenery-from a virtual cockpit interior to a movie-like exterior view-is smoothly streamed in high quality right from Microsoft's servers. Such seamless flight made Flight Simulator attract over two million players within weeks after the release and seal its instant-classic position.

CHAPTER 9
TRAINING AND LEARNING MODULES

Ready to get started learning to fly with a flight simulator? You've come to the right place.

In this post, you'll find the ultimate resource for flight sim training-from virtual flight school add-ons to online lessons.

We'll take a look at a mixture of free and paid tools to help you build your flying skills with realism and confidence. Moreover, we show you how simulators can be an excellent way to prepare for flight school.

Starting with free options like YouTube

Looking to enhance your flight simulator skills? YouTube is a fantastic starting point, offering free tutorials on nearly every flying topic imaginable.

Popular YouTube Channels for Flight Sim Training

Here are some standout channels led by real airline pilots and aviation experts:

- **AviationPro**: Hosted by a Boeing 777 & 787 pilot; this channel focuses on airliner operations and VATSIM tutorials.
- **flightdeck2sim:** Step-by-step tutorials with explanations from a Boeing 737 captain and type rating instructor.
- **320 Sim Pilot:** In-depth step-by-step tutorial video from an Airbus A320 pilot.

Curious about general aviation? Follow the YouTube channel PilotEdge, with in-depth videos on ATC/ communication and airspace training focused on GA pilots.

For in-depth flights into the real world of flight, follow these YouTube Channels, as they barely ever fly simulators:

- Angle of Attack
- Boldmethod
- MzeroA Flight Training

And then, of course, there is the **Flight Sim Coach** YouTube channel, filled with sim tips and recordings of live lessons with certified flight instructors.

YouTube: Great but Not Perfect

While YouTube's content is free, some videos are more about entertaining than educating. Plus, you won't get personalized feedback or guidance-pretty important when trying to master flying skills.

Online Flying Lessons with Real Instructors ($60–$80/hr)

This is what you get when you fly with a live Certified Flight Instructor (CFI) who teaches you as you fly your simulator. With online lessons, you will receive real-time feedback tailored to your needs.

Here's how it works:

Share your screen via Zoom and he'll be able to see your cockpit and provide on-screen diagrams or notes.

Employ more advanced features through FSC Link, which allows the instructor to see hidden controls-rudder and trim-and even simulate system failures or changes in weather.

Why Choose One-on-One Lessons?

A truly experienced instructor corrects bad habits, like over-reliance on instruments, that sim users frequently pick up. Ground-school material is current as are the latest rules and testing standards, offering lots of value regarding situational awareness, risk management, and real-world tools such as ForeFlight.

While these tools are helpful, they'll never replace the value brought about by a tailored real instructor-particularly one acquainted with your aircraft and your region.

If you're serious about improving your flight skills, personalized lessons are an investment that truly pays off.

Flight Sim Enthusiasts

Enjoy a Personalized Lesson from a Real Citation Pilot

Have you ever wondered how it would feel to fly an RNAV (RNP) approach in a Cessna Citation CJ4? Imagine learning from an experienced instructor who makes sure every single detail is spot on and will keep pushing you further into your virtual pilot career.

Our instructors tailor lessons to your interests and skill level, adapting on the fly to what you need most.

Want to sharpen your ATC communication for confident flying on VATSIM? We've got you covered.

Curious about the inner workings of airline operations? Fly alongside a real 737 pilot and get answers to all your burning questions.

Sim Setup and Tech Support

Our instructors aren't just pilots; they're also tech-savvy sim enthusiasts. Whether you need help troubleshooting a setup issue, guidance on your next hardware or software purchase, or assistance configuring your simulator, they're ready to help.

More engaging, immersive, and hugely motivating, all this comes with learning with a real person. Added to that would be personalized support, which no computer is capable of giving.

This service is available for real-world pilots and/or simulator hobbyists all over the world, whether you are a newcomer or experienced in aviation.

BUILT-IN FLIGHT LESSONS AND TUTORIALS [FREE]

Microsoft Flight Simulator (MSFS) features a set of in-game tutorials that will teach you the basics of flying. Here's what you can learn from them:

Basic Controls & Cameras: Learn your surroundings and how to navigate around the cockpit.

Attitudes & Instruments: Learn the basics of managing flight.

Takeoff & Level Flight: Learn to lift off smoothly and maintain a steady flight.

Landing: Practice techniques for a successful touchdown.

Traffic Patterns: Maneuver safely around airfields, even in busy skies.

First Solo Flight: Handle a traffic pattern entirely on your own.

Navigation: Follow a flight plan from point A to point B.

First Solo Navigation: Execute a solo flight from point A to point B.

The training will be in the Cessna 152, a very good trainer aircraft with simple controls and easy-to-read panels. Training is provided at Sedona Airport (KSEZ), one of the most beautifully surrounded airports in the United States. On the downside, the tabletop nature of this airport makes judgment of height rather difficult.

Pros and Cons MSFS Flight Lessons

What's Great

- The virtual instructor is friendly and approachable, making the experience enjoyable.
- It covers essential skills that provide a solid foundation for beginners.

What Could Be Better

- The instructions are basic and don't adjust to your performance. For instance, if you stall during landing, the instructor might not even mention it.
- Visual aids are restricted to simple graphics, which may not work well for those who learn best through visuals.
- While the lessons explain what to do, they don't dive into the how or why, which can leave gaps in understanding.

Overall, these tutorials are a great starting point for beginners but may leave advanced learners craving more detailed feedback and guidance.

Learning the Basics in MSFS and X-Plane

Microsoft Flight Simulator (MSFS)

The first few lessons in MSFS are a good primer to learn the basic controls, keyboard shortcuts, and fundamental flying techniques. They are perfect for familiarizing yourself with the interface and mechanics of the simulator.

However, if you're looking to deeply understand what you're doing, refine your skills, or transition to more complex aircraft, these lessons may feel somewhat limited.

X-Plane

X-Plane offers a built-in flight school with a step-by-step approach, providing instructions via text and basic graphics (no voice guidance).

Key Features:

Lessons simplify the tasks for the beginner by limiting some of the controls until you get used to them. For instance, in turning exercises, the elevator is locked so you will only have to worry about that task.

Keyboard shortcuts relevant to your progress are gradually introduced to ease use of the simulator.

There are three major categories of lessons:

1. General Aviation: Covering basic operations of the aircraft, such as takeoffs, landings, traffic patterns, and procedures for flying taildraggers in aircraft like the SR-22, Cessna 172, and Stinson L5.

2. Navigation: Describes some VOR navigation and some ILS approaches.

3. Helicopters: The very basics of helicopters, covered with the Sikorsky S-76C.

Visuals:

While X-Plane contains some visualization aids regarding some concepts, such as how VOR radials work, the text-heavy and sometimes sparse instructions of concepts may make it hard to understand for a sharp-visual learner.

Feedback:

You receive an after-certain-lesson report card with numerical scores on how you did.

Mobile Version:

Even the mobile version of X-Plane includes a flight school, making it an incredibly affordable and portable way to learn the basics using a robust simulator on your phone or tablet.

Bottom Line:

Both MSFS and X-Plane are excellent starting points for beginners. MSFS is more user-friendly for very casual learning, while in X-Plane, a methodical approach is in place, perfect for people wanting to delve deeper into aviation basics.

X-Plane Mobile Version

After completing certain lessons in X-Plane, you'll receive a report card with numerical scores to track your progress.

If you're looking for an affordable way to start learning, the mobile version of X-Plane includes flight school functionality, offering a great way to practice basic skills with a powerful simulator right on your phone or tablet.

Prepar3D

Unlike other simulators, Prepar3D does not have in-game flight lessons. You can, however, complement your learning through other resources like remote instruction or add-ons such as FSFlyingSchool.

FSX (Microsoft Flight Simulator X)

If you have FSX, you will be able to take a lesson from one of the most experienced flying instructors around: Rod Machado. As his name may suggest, Rod's lessons are known to be a bit hilarious and has introduced a number of pilots to their first flights. If you already have FSX, you can definitely start with trying a lesson from him.

Flight Sim Training Add-Ons

Both X-Plane and Microsoft Flight Simulator (MSFS) have additional training add-ons available that extend the functionality beyond the basic lessons. These add-ons offer more aircraft, detailed lessons, and higher quality content.

While these add-ons won't offer the interactive feedback of a live instructor, they still offer an affordable and valuable way to continue your flight training in the simulator.

Flight School Tutorials

Learning to Fly with Flight Simulators

These days, learning to fly does not have to be about hopping into a real aircraft with an instructor. Modern flight simulators provide safe, controlled, and incredibly realistic ways to learn the nuts and bolts of flying. If you're considering a pilot's license, grasping these tools and their purpose in flight training will give you a head start.

What Are Flight Simulators?

Flight simulators are computer-based systems designed to simulate real-life flying experiences. Unlike video games, these simulators focus on realism to enhance learning.

They help aspiring pilots practice aircraft controls, interact with air traffic controllers, and adapt to varying weather conditions and scenarios, preparing them for real-world flight challenges.

TYPES OF FLIGHT SIMULATORS

At-Home Flight Simulators

At-home simulators vary in complexity:

Basic Models: These have realistic controls, ideal for beginners in aviation or those on a tight budget.

Intermediate Models: These are equipped with pilot-style seats and screen displays, ideal for flight school students who want additional practice.

Advanced Models: These are high-end simulators with motion capability and professional-grade components; the experience they offer will be just about as real as flight school setups.

FAA-Approved Simulators

BATD (Basic Aviation Training Device): These simulators mimic real aircraft with accurate controls, displays, and performance characteristics like stall speeds and climb rates, meeting FAA standards for initial pilot training.

AATD (Advanced Aviation Training Device): More sophisticated than BATDs, AATDs feature GPS, visual systems, and emergency procedure simulations, meeting stricter FAA guidelines.

FFS stands for Full Flight Simulator: These represent the pinnacle of realism: for professional pilots, it includes a motion platform, actual sounds, and advanced modeling of the aircraft's aerodynamics. These are used in the training of pilots on particular aircraft or to satisfy requirements for recurrent training.

FTD (Flight Training Device): Similar to FFS models, FTD simulators focus on specific aircraft training. They include enclosed cockpits and lifelike visual displays but may lack full motion simulation. Airlines often use FTDs for training on older aircraft models or for flight certification.

How Accurate Are Flight Simulators?

The accuracy of a simulator depends on its type:

At-Home Models: Good for learning the basics, but they lack the precision needed for advanced training.

FAA-Approved Simulators: These are so realistic that flight hours logged on them often count toward official flight requirements. For example, simulators such as those at JA Flight School are accurate enough to replicate real flying with seamless ease.

Flight simulators have brought a complete revolution in the field of aviation training due to their affordability, accessibility, and safety. Be it a novice taking his maiden flight or an experienced pilot needing to hone his skills further, there is a type of simulator available for your needs.

How "Real" Is the Feel in a Flight Simulator?

Some have argued whether the concept of "real feel" with regard to flight simulators provides a realistic sensation that immerses you into lifelike controls, visuals, and motion. There are times when feeling the sensation of takeoff and landing and flying through different types of weather can enhance your training. A totally realistic "real feel" is difficult to provide. Even the most advanced simulator cannot accurately simulate all motions of an aircraft. In addition, they can also create "false motion cues," or sensations that a pilot would not encounter in an actual flight. When choosing a simulator, one has to look beyond the motion effect itself: factors such as visuals, control accuracy, and the design and model of the simulator itself play a critical role.

Challenges of Flight Simulator Training

Even flight simulators have a few shortcomings:

Lack of Full Realism: No simulator, regardless of quality, can perfectly match the experience of flying a real aircraft. To become a proficient pilot, you'll need real-world flight hours to adapt to dynamic conditions and emergencies.

Limited Self-Training: At-home simulators are excellent for practice but cannot replace professional training. Feedback from an experienced instructor is crucial for improving your skills and ensuring safety.

Advantages of Flight Simulator Training

Despite their shortcomings, flight simulators enjoy certain decided advantages:

Safety First: Simulators let you practice complex maneuvers and emergency responses without risk.

Cost-Effective: They lessen the need for expensive hours of flying an actual aircraft.

Versatility: Simulators can allow you to train under different conditions, from various weather scenarios to unique challenges in flight.

Licensing Support: Time spent in FAA-approved simulators can count toward the hours needed to earn your pilot's license.

Building skills safely and inexpensively, using a flight simulator as part of your training is smart. For professional guidance in hands-on experience, combining simulator practice with real flights and instructor feedback is the best way. If you're ready to elevate your training, our state-of-the-art simulators are here to help.

ENHANCING SKILLS WITH AI ASSISTANCE

AI Compatibility with Microsoft Flight Simulator 2024

Mark your calendars for November 19th when Microsoft Flight Simulator 2024 takes to the skies, and SayIntentions.AI will be ready on day one. Through early access via the Tech Alpha and Dev Alpha builds courtesy of a trusted partner, we have extensively tested our tools to ensure a seamless experience for virtual pilots at launch.

We're not only ensuring compatibility but also embracing new and enhanced features of MSFS 2024 to provide an even more immersive and realistic flight simulation experience. Stay tuned to take your virtual aviation to the next level!

Primary Access Testing

Delivering Excellence from Day One

With rigorous testing during the Tech and Dev Alpha phases, we've identified and resolved critical performance areas ahead of Microsoft Flight Simulator 2024's (MSFS 2024) release. This proactive approach ensures that **SayIntentions.AI** integrates seamlessly with the new simulator, providing precise and reliable ATC interactions from the very start.

Be it complicated airspace or a VFR flight for scenic pleasures, rest assured our software will do great service and enhance your flying experience.

Accommodating MSFS 2024's "Living World"

MSFS 2024 is introducing such features as detailed offshore rigs and heliports that make this simulation environment dynamic and interactive. In turn, SayIntentions.AI develops specialized radio communications for offshore and remote operations.

This will give pilots realistic and accurate interactions while flying to oil rigs or heliports, adding immersion and realism to your flights. We are working to make the simulator as close to real life as possible, and we want your experience to be as good as it can be.

Help Shape the Future

At SayIntentions.AI, we're committed to innovation and value your input in shaping our updates for MSFS 2024. Through our Partner Program, we're inviting our most passionate users to preview new features, share feedback, and influence the development process.

Our first post-launch priority is the refinement of operational communications for oil rigs and heliports, ensuring that they reflect real-world standards. Your insights will help us to fine-tune these features before they're released to all users.

Partner Program Highlights:

Early Access: See major updates, including features specific to MSFS 2024 such as Traffic Injection.

Testing Opportunities: Gain access to our Experimental server to test the latest tools.

Roadmap Input: Vote for feature priorities.

Exclusive Perks: Receive a "Partner" role in Discord with special perks.

Swag Packs: Get exclusive items among other rewards where shipping is available.

While partners are instrumental in accelerating development, all users will benefit from these innovations. Features introduced via the Partner Program will roll out to the entire community on our regular schedule, ensuring everyone enjoys the improved radio communications and cutting-edge tools. This collaborative approach enables us to deliver faster, higher-quality updates while maintaining exceptional standards for all SayIntentions.AI users.

CERTIFICATION CHALLENGES AND ACHIEVEMENTS

Every accomplishment in Microsoft Flight Simulator 2024

Achievements in Microsoft Flight Simulator 2024

Beginner Moments:

First Flight: Finish a flight in any mode.

Baby Steps: Complete your first training mission in a tutorial.

Amateur Photographer: Take a snapshot in World Photographer using the photo mode.

Photography Enthusiast:

Say Three: Take three 3-star photos in different World Photographer collections.

Scrapbooking: Complete a Collection Page in World Photographer.

Extended Portfolio: Complete 10 Collection Pages.

Versatile Photography: Complete a Collection Page in Aviation, Man-Made, Nature, and Fauna categories.

Sky Full of Stars: Collect 100 Stars in World Photographer.

Exploration and Adventure:

Skyward Sightseer: Hover near 7 landmarks by hot-air balloon for at least 3 minutes each.

Wind Whisperer: Glide for a total of 20 minutes.

5K Fun Run: Walk or run 5 kilometers in the game.

Give Us a Wave: Make 30 perfect seaplane landings.

Pilot Skill Challenges:

Aced It: Get an A grade in any Training mission outside of Career mode.

Touch & Go: Carry out two touch-and-go landings at two different airports in one session.

Eclectic Eagle: Fly for 2 hours each in a jet, airliner, glider, and rotorcraft.

On Your Way: Buildup 50 hours of flight time.

Helo Hero: Land successfully at 50 heliports without incident.

Competitive Spirit:

Multi-talented: Reach a rank in every weekly Challenge in Challenge League.

Challenger: Complete 10 weekly Challenges.

Thrillseeker: Complete 100 weekly Challenges.

Career Achievements:

- **Overachiever**: Unlock all 20 base certifications in the Career mode.
- **Earning Your Wings**: Get your Private Pilot's License in Career mode.
- **Growing the Fleet**: Buy 5 aircraft in the Career.
- **Entrepreneurial Spirit**: Start your first company in Career mode.

Jack-of-All-Trades:

Jack of All Trades: Complete 3 missions each in World Photographer, Career, and Challenge League.

Your Own Private Pilot: Take off from one airport and land at another in an aircraft you own.

CHAPTER 10
USING VIRTUAL REALITY AND IMMERSIVE TOOLS

Since its 2020 debut, Microsoft Flight Simulator has seen a few updates-including a new naming scheme for the 2024 release. The actual core gameplay hasn't changed much: flying real aircraft around a beautiful 3D recreation of Earth.

Shortly after its release, VR support was added to the game, and that seems to be a feature of future updates. While already an amazing experience, actually flying through this detailed simulation, stepping into the cockpit with a VR headset elevates the experience to a totally new level.

Microsoft officially supports a range of VR headsets from PC-focused brands such as Valve and HP. However, standalone headsets, like those from Meta, also work seamlessly thanks to their PC VR integration that makes the simulation more accessible than ever. Below, you will find my top recommendations for the best VR headsets to elevate your Flight Simulator experience.

How to choose the right VR headset

My go-to headset for playing Microsoft Flight Simulator in VR is still the Meta Quest 3. Meta is still the leader when it comes to virtual reality hardware and software, and the Quest 3 is proof of that innovation. This isn't just a PC VR gaming headset; it's a full-color mixed reality headset with passthrough cameras that allow for seamless, cable-free play. Whether you're powered solely by the headset or using it to navigate your simulation setup, it helps you position flight sticks, pedals, and other gear with ease.

Nicholas Sutrich at Android Central aptly called it "the best VR headset you can buy" in his Meta Quest 3 review, and I couldn't agree more. It works with PC VR using either a USB-C cable or wirelessly via Air Link, but you'll need a Wi-Fi 6 router or higher to do so. Not to be outdone by itself, the Quest 3 is comfortable to wear while wearing it, and the improved lenses provide a much sharper experience compared to its predecessor. While it's pricier than the Quest 2, it's the most accessible and best overall VR headset for both gamers and simulation enthusiasts alike, making it ideal for titles like *Euro Truck Simulator 2 and *Microsoft Flight Simulator.

The headset boasts a resolution of 2064 x 2208 per eye, a 110-degree field of view (FOV), and an adjustable interpupillary distance (IPD) range of 58–71 mm. The IPD adjustment is done using a physical wheel with digital readout, and much more fine-grained than Quest 2's three-notch system. My IPD is about 66 mm and I find this new mechanism far better. For top-of-the-line, standalone VR solution for Microsoft Flight Simulator, Meta Quest 3 is in a class of its own.

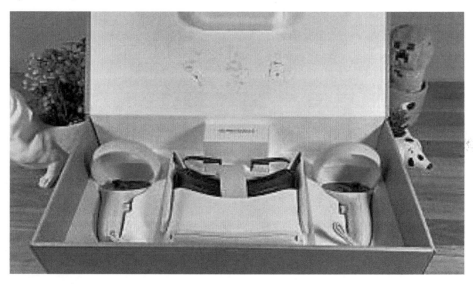

Unboxing a Meta Quest 2. Image credit: Ben Wilson | Windows Central

Microsoft Flight Simulator is already a very advanced game, but with a VR headset, it gets even better. Instead of just viewing the action on a monitor, VR puts you inside the cockpit-for real-viewing the cockpit and the world as you fly around the globe. However, enabling VR can increase the game's already demanding hardware requirements.

If your gaming setup needs an upgrade to handle the additional load, consider checking out the best pre-built gaming PCs or gaming laptops optimized for *Flight Simulator*.

Of course, any of these recommended VR headsets will be a great experience, but the last-generation Meta Quest 2 is an affordable way for beginners to get into the action. It combines quality visuals, immersive audio, precise controls, and reliable tracking to create a memorable VR experience. For those just starting, it's an excellent way to explore VR gaming, and it might even inspire you to upgrade your gear down the line.

SETTING UP VR FOR MSFS 2024

Microsoft Flight Simulator 2024 is gearing up to deliver an exceptional VR experience. Developers have emphasized VR improvements for this edition, and the stunning new planes and locations look even more breathtaking in virtual reality. Headsets like the Pimax Crystal Light are set to make these enhancements truly shine.

What You'll Find Below:

- Optimized VR Settings for MSFS 2024 by GPU
- Best Accessories for MSFS 2024 in VR
- Why MSFS 2024 is Perfect for VR Enthusiasts

Dive in to explore how you can make the most of your VR flights in this next-level simulator!

Best VR Settings for Microsoft Flight Simulator 2024 (MSFS2024) by GPU

Optimization of both in-game and PC settings is crucial for a smooth and realistic VR experience in MSFS2024. VR is very demanding on hardware, and even the tiniest tweaks can greatly improve performance and visual quality.

Why Optimization Matters:

1. Efficient Resource Management: VR uses a lot of processing power, graphics capabilities, and memory. Tuning your settings ensures your system allocates these resources efficiently.

2. Minimizing Stuttering and Lag: Unoptimized settings may cause lag and stutter, which disrupt the VR experience and may cause discomfort or disorientation.

3. Improved Visual Quality: This balance between performance and visuals gives leeway in enhancing the game's view while not compromising frame rates.

4. Extended Laptop Battery Life: Optimization removes stress from the system components, which in turn makes it easier on laptops and helps conserve battery power while playing games.

Key Settings to Tweak:

1. Graphics Presets: Start with a lower preset and gradually increase based on your system's performance.

2. Render Scale: Adjust the resolution—lowering this can boost performance but reduces visual clarity.

3. Texture Quality: Lower settings reduce memory usage, improving performance while keeping acceptable detail.

4. Object Level of Detail (LOD): Decrease LOD to improve frame rates in dense environments without compromising too much on visuals.

5. VSync: Reduces screen tearing but can introduce input lag. Test to see if it improves your setup.

PC-Specific Adjustments:

Power Settings: Switch to high-performance mode on your PC for better hardware output.

Driver Updates: Always use the latest GPU drivers for improved compatibility and performance.

Overclocking: If comfortable, do so with your GPU and CPU to gain more power, but do ensure stability.

Step-by-Step VR Optimization for GPUs

Nvidia Users:

1. Launch the Nvidia Control Panel, then click on 3D Settings.

2. Under Image Sharpening, set this to 0.25. This setting greatly improves the sharpness of faraway objects.

These optimizations will indeed make your VR experience smoother and far more captivating in Microsoft Flight Simulator 2024, whatever your hardware setup may be.

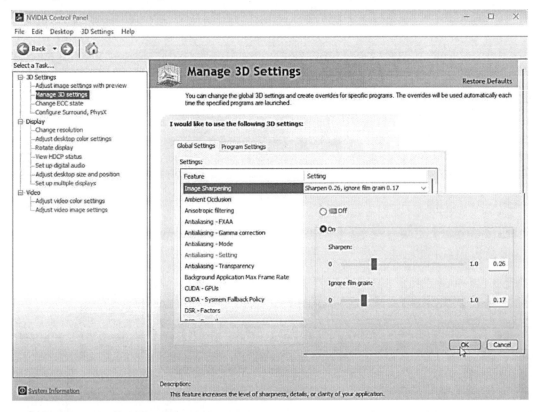

Next, scroll down and set the Power Management Mode to Prefer Maximum Performance to ensure your system delivers its best during gameplay. Don't forget to hit Apply to save the changes!

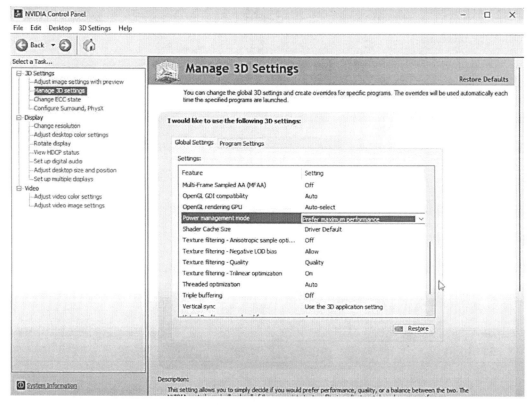

Step 2: Adjust the Pimax Play refresh rate to 120 Hz.

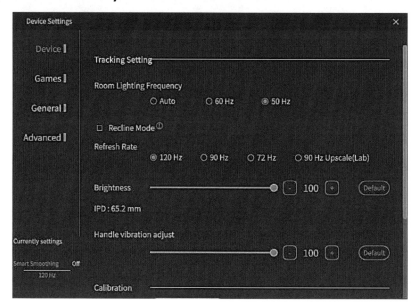

Keep the Render Quality set to High and Fixed Foveated Rendering set to Balanced.

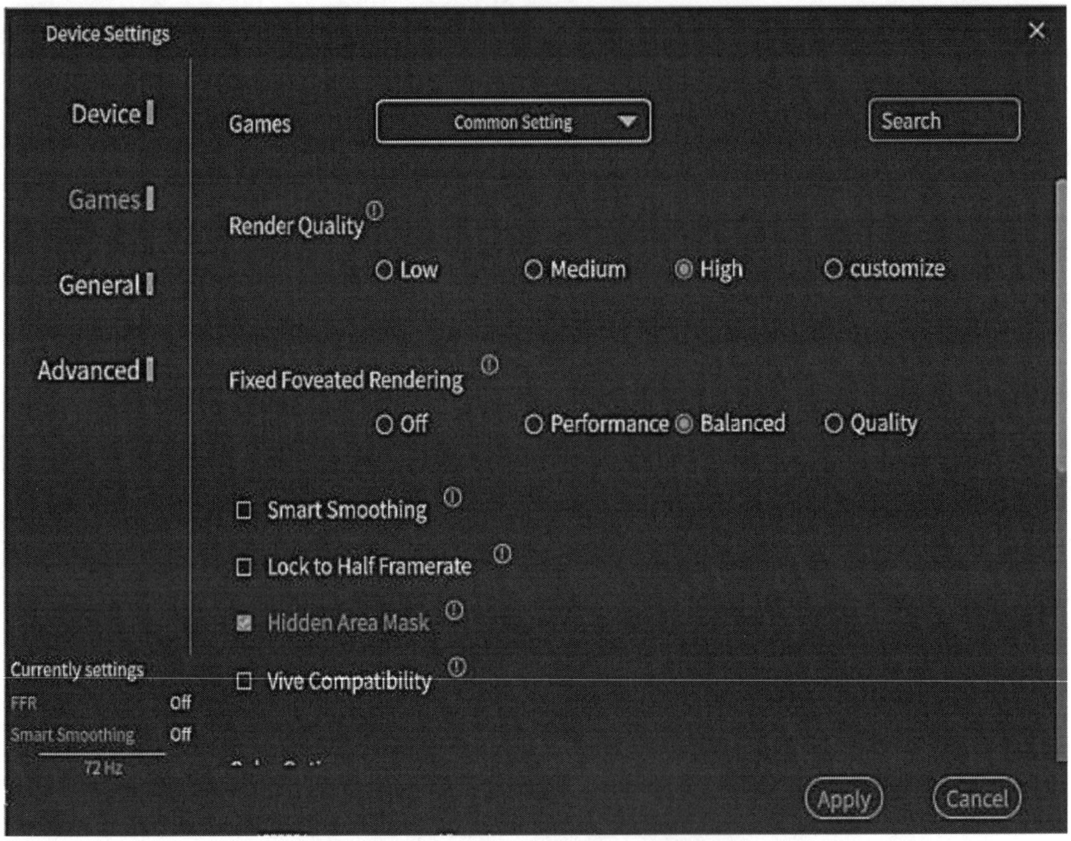

Step 3

In PimaxXR, make sure "Lock to Half Framerate" is enabled.

Step 4: RTX 4090 Settings

If you have an RTX 4090 card, the following are the steps to complete:

In Microsoft Flight Simulator, using the OpenXR Toolkit, enable Fixed Foveated Rendering. Press Ctrl + F2 to open on-screen display.

Outer Ring Size should be changed to 60% for best results.

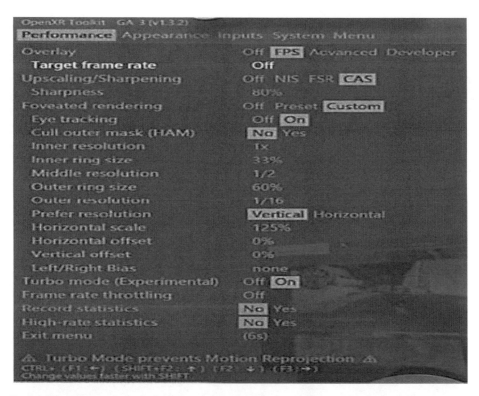

Next, adjust the settings as shown in the reference image:

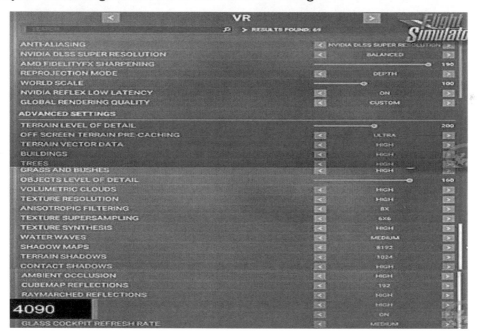

For the RTX 4060 Ti and RTX 3080, the following settings are recommended:

1. Launch Microsoft Flight Simulator and enable Fixed Foveated Rendering via the on-screen display menu of the OpenXR Toolkit. You can open the menu by pressing Ctrl + F2.

2. Set the Outer Ring Size to 50% for the best performance and balanced appearance.

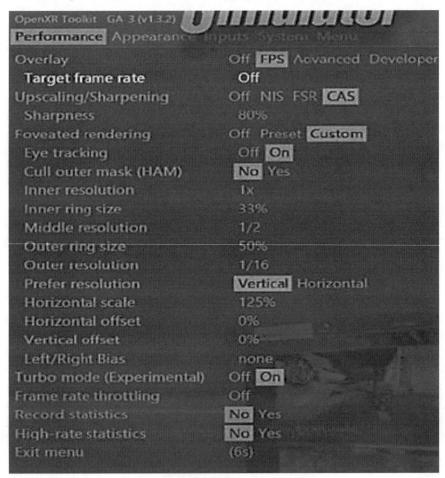

Next, adjust the settings as shown in the reference image:

ANTI-ALIASING		NVIDIA DLSS SUPER RESOLUTION
NVIDIA DLSS SUPER RESOLUTION		BALANCED
AMD FIDELITYFX SHARPENING		190
REPROJECTION MODE		DEPTH
WORLD SCALE		100
NVIDIA REFLEX LOW LATENCY		ON
GLOBAL RENDERING QUALITY		CUSTOM
ADVANCED SETTINGS		
TERRAIN LEVEL OF DETAIL		130
OFF SCREEN TERRAIN PRE-CACHING		ULTRA
TERRAIN VECTOR DATA		MEDIUM
BUILDINGS		MEDIUM
TREES		MEDIUM
GRASS AND BUSHES		MEDIUM
OBJECTS LEVEL OF DETAIL		100
VOLUMETRIC CLOUDS		MEDIUM
TEXTURE RESOLUTION		HIGH
ANISOTROPIC FILTERING		8X
TEXTURE SUPERSAMPLING		6X6
TEXTURE SYNTHESIS		HIGH
WATER WAVES		MEDIUM
SHADOW MAPS		8192
TERRAIN SHADOWS		1024
CONTACT SHADOWS		HIGH
WINDSHIELD EFFECTS		HIGH
AMBIENT OCCLUSION		HIGH
CUBEMAP REFLECTIONS		192
RAYMARCHED REFLECTIONS		HIGH
RTX 4060 TI		HIGH
RTX 3080		ON
GLASS COCKPIT REFRESH RATE		MEDIUM

RTX 3060 Ti Configuration:

To optimize settings for the RTX 3060 Ti, perform the following:

1. Open the OpenXR Toolkit onscreen display in MSFS using Ctrl + F2.

2. Turn off Fixed Foveated Rendering.

3. Set the Outer Ring Size to 50%.

4. Set the Middle Resolution to 1/4.

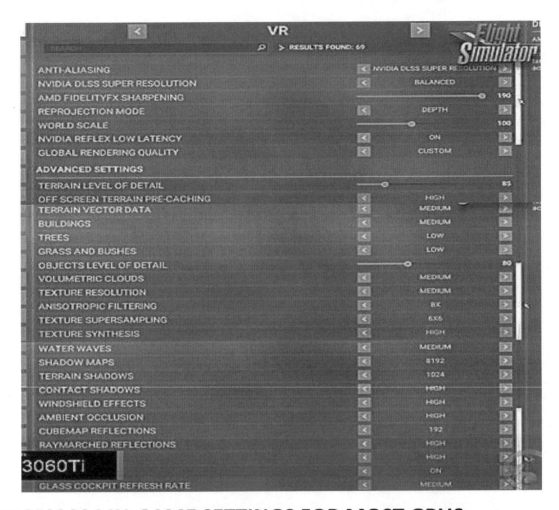

MSFS2024 IN-GAME SETTINGS FOR MOST GPUS

Here are the optimal settings for smooth performance across most GPUs:

- **Render Scaling**: 80% (adjustable for quality)
- **Global Render Quality:** Medium
- **Anti-Aliasing:** TAA (can be turned off)
- **Terrain LoD:** 85%
- **Terrain Vector**: Data Low
- **Objects LoD**: 85%
- **Windshield Effects:** High
- **Ambient Occlusion**: Off (important for performance)
- **Volumetric Clouds:** Low
- **Texture Resolution**: Medium

- **Anisotropic Filtering:** 16x (can lower if needed)
- **Texture Supersampling:** 4x4 (if needed, lower)
- **Texture Synthesis:** High (impacts sharpness of textures at a distance)
- **Water Waves:** High
- **Shadow Maps**: 768
- **Terrain Shadows:** Off
- **Contact Shadows**: Off
- **Reflections:** Low
- **Light Shafts**: Off
- **Bloom**: Off
- **Depth of Field**: Off
- **Lens Correction**: Off
- **Lens Flare**: Off
- **Cockpit Refresh Rate**: Low
- **Building**s: High
- **Trees:** Medium
- **Grass and Bushes:** Medium

MINIMUM PC REQUIREMENTS FOR MSFS2024 IN VR

You need a strong gaming computer to run MSFS 2024 smoothly in VR. Recommended specs are as follows:

- CPU: AMD Ryzen 7 5800X or Intel Core i7-12700K (or equivalent)
- GPU: NVIDIA RTX 3080 or AMD Radeon RX 6800 XT (or similar)
- RAM: 32GB DDR4 or DDR5
- Storage: SSD, preferably NVMe

Best VR Headsets for MSFS2024

The best VR headsets depend on your budget for VR:

Budget Option - Pimax Crystal Light

- **Price:** Starting $699
- **Resolution:** 2880 x 2880 per eye
- Glass aspheric lenses ensure that the graphics are crystal clear with 35 PPD.
- Clarity in high fidelity dash: 17 million pixels.

Premium Option-Pimax Crystal Super:

- World's first interchangeable optical engine, QLED & micro-OLED
- Resolution: 3840 x 3840 pixels per eye
- Eye tracking

MSFS2024 Essential Accessories in VR:

Following are some accessories that one may consider to enhance their experience:

Flight Sim Yoke: This is great for aircraft control.

Flight Sim Throttles: For power and speed management.

Rudders: These are used to simulate real aircraft pedals.

Headset Stand: Keep your headset stored and protected when not in use.

Controller Charging Station: Keep controllers powered.

Comfort Strap: To improve headset comfort

Lens Inserts: To prevent lens scratches

Cooling Fans: Attach to your VR headset for comfort during long sessions

By investing in the right hardware and accessories, you'll enjoy a highly immersive and realistic flight simulation experience in VR.

WHY MSFS 2024 IS A GREAT VR CHOICE

Microsoft Flight Simulator 2024 is going to be an exceptional VR experience, and here's why:

Designed with VR in Mind: MSFS 2024 is built from scratch for virtual reality, meaning its mechanics, controls, and visuals are optimized for immersive VR play.

Smarter Performance: Smoother frame rates and lower latency will make the VR experience in MSFS 2024 much more comfortable, with minimal chances of motion sickness.

Stunning Visuals: With better graphics technology, the game promises to be a visual treat in VR, making the virtual world look almost real.

Realistic Lighting and Shadows: Advanced light and shadow effects are introduced in the game, adding to the visual realism of the virtual environment.

Native VR Support: MSFS 2024 will most likely include native VR support that eliminates any need for third-party mods or tools, which ensures smooth VR gameplay.

Immersive Gameplay: Given the commitment by Microsoft towards creating engaging experiences, MSFS 2024's VR version should arguably deliver a far more engaging and immersive flying experience.

Although more details may emerge closer to release, these improvements suggest that MSFS 2024 will deliver a much more polished VR experience compared to its predecessor.

IMMERSIVE COCKPIT EXPERIENCES

Discover the Ultimate Flight Simulation Experience: A Partnership with Microsoft Flight Simulator

Buckle up for a thrilling takeoff as we unveil an exciting partnership with Microsoft Flight Simulator, one of the most immersive and iconic flight simulation platforms in the world. We are pleased to introduce a new licensed product, designed for aviation enthusiasts and aspiring pilots, which raises your flight experience to completely new altitudes.

The core of this cooperation is a brand-new seat design, specially created for long flights in the virtual world of MSFS2024. Ergonomic excellence combined with premium materials will guarantee maximum comfort and support during extended simulation sessions. Be it a long flight over continents or the discovery of new skies, this seat takes realism and immersion to the next level.

We're excited to team up with the Microsoft Flight Simulator team to create this game-changing product," said Kam Khadem, CMO of Next Level Racing. "Together, we're delivering an unparalleled immersive experience for the flight simulation community. We can't wait to connect with our audience through upcoming events and activations to show them exactly how this partnership is going to take their simulation like never before.

This product is due to be released in Q1 2025, giving enthusiasts something to look forward to as they prepare for the next era of flight simulation.

Want to be the first to know?

We invite all aviation enthusiasts to register for exclusive updates and early access. Joining our community means you will be the first to know when this exciting launch is announced, including features and availability.

ENHANCING GAMEPLAY WITH THIRD-PARTY TOOLS

Game Mode

To start, go to the search bar, type "Game Mode," and select "Game Mode settings." Toggle off Game Mode. Many experts recommend leaving Game Mode off, even though there isn't a lot of concrete evidence against it. Afterward, under "Related Settings," you'll see an option for "Graphics." Click on it and look for programs like Microsoft Flight Simulator or X-Plane. Select the program and click "Options." Choose the "High performance" setting and click Save. This new feature is often suggested by experts for optimal performance.

HAGS (Hardware-accelerated GPU Scheduling)

For the best performance and quality with NVIDIA's 4000 series cards, you'll need to enable HAGS, which is also required for new DLSS and frame generation technologies. For this, head to the "Graphics" page-the search bar should have "Graphics" for quick access-or simply click on "Change default graphics settings" and flip "Hardware-accelerated GPU scheduling" ON. Also, enable "Optimizations for windowed games." If you have an older GPU, such as from the 2000 or 3000 series, you may want to keep HAGS disabled, but feel free to experiment to find what works best for you.

Windows Defender

Search for "Windows Security" and click on it. Then, in "Virus & threat protection," under "Virus & threat protection settings," click "Manage settings." Scroll down to "Exclusions," select "Add or remove exclusions," and click "Add an exclusion." In the dropdown, select "Folder" and select the install directory of your simulator. This will prevent Windows Defender from using processing power to scan your game while you're flying. If you use Steam for games like MSFS2020 you can exclude the entire Steam folder. Defender is enough to keep your PC safe without slowing it down.

Nvidia Drivers

If you have an Nvidia card, it is a good idea to keep your drivers up to date. In the flight sim community, Nvidia has been the go-to choose for many years due to its quality and performance, though some gamers have started to prefer Ryzen. Upgrade to the latest drivers; ideally, these should be less than a year old. When upgrading, select the "Custom Installation" option and check the "Perform a clean installation" box to remove old drivers and install the latest ones.

Nvidia Control Panel or Other GPU Interface

Make sure your primary graphics card is set to be the default. For instance, on my laptop, I use the Nvidia Control Panel to make my 4090 the default card for gaming and simulations, overriding the internal GPU. Simulations cannot be displayed on internal graphics processors. This is primarily a concern with laptops. In my experience, adjusting Nvidia settings beyond default generally does nothing to enhance either performance or quality. The only setting I may ever change is to make sure that the maximum performance is always on, but even on default, the GPU switches to high performance when necessary. After years of testing, I've found that often the least amount of tweaking produces the best overall performance.

Removing Bloatware

The best thing I do for my system is to get rid of unnecessary programs that bog it down, such as third-party antivirus software. It's not needed and can cause performance issues along with slowing down the system. Windows Defender does an excellent job on its own. First, you'll want to search for "Add or remove programs" in the search bar and open it. From there, go through that list and uninstall everything, such as McAfee and Norton antivirus, Microsoft Office - it's such a resource hog - and those other programs that you, the flight simmer, won't need. You see, years ago, viruses used to be a big fear, but they are quite minimal these days. I was finding computers running slow and almost unresponsive because of this antivirus program and that antivirus program, so I just remove them these days. Only take care not to delete any file critical to Windows or which may be required later.

CHAPTER 11
CUSTOMIZATION AND MODDING

How to Install Mods in Microsoft Flight Simulator

Mods are custom content created by the community to enhance your Microsoft Flight Simulator experience.

How to Install Mods

To install mods, you need to place the files into the "Community" folder.

Default Installation Locations:

Microsoft Store/Xbox App:

C:\\Users\\YourUsername\\AppData\\Local\\Packages\\Microsoft.FlightSimulator_8wekyb3d8bbwe Steam:

\\LocalCache\\Packages\\Community

  C:\\Users\\YourUsername\\AppData\\Roaming\\Microsoft Flight Simulator\\Packages\\Community

Note: The "AppData" folder is hidden by default in Windows 10/11. To see it, you need to go to the "View" tab in File Explorer, and then check the box that says "Hidden items."

If You Can't See Your Mod in the Simulator

Make sure the mod is installed properly. Open the mod folder in the "Community" folder, and ensure that the "manifest.json" and "layout.json" files are in the root of the mod folder.

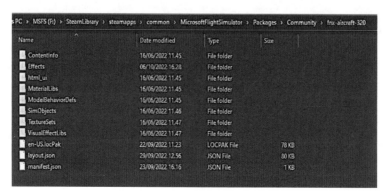

To make sure the mod is installed in the correct "Community" folder, check if you have installed the simulator in a custom location. If so, there will be a "Community" folder in that custom directory as well as one in your C:\Users\YourUsername location.

To verify the correct path:

1. Go to C:\Users\YourUsername\AppData\....

2. Find the UserCfg.opt file and open it with Notepad.

3. Scroll to the bottom and check the "InstalledPackagesPath." For example:

   `InstalledPackagesPath "F:\SteamLibrary\steamapps\common\MicrosoftFlightSimulator\Packages"`

   This is where the simulator looks for mods. If it's incorrect, you can manually update it and save the file.

If you can't find the "Community" folder, follow these steps:

1. Launch Microsoft Flight Simulator.

2. Go to Options > General Options > Developers, and turn on "Developer Mode."

3. Open the Developer Toolbar> Tools > Virtual File System > Packages Folders, then click on "Open Community Folder."

This will show you the correct location where the simulator reads for mods, as indicated in the UserCfg.opt file.

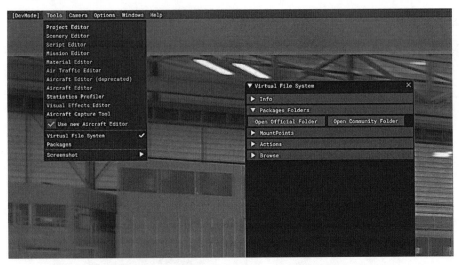

Some mods may require special steps for installation. Please stick to the particular instructions of the mod's creators for the best results.

Important Warning

Mods are not official products of Microsoft Flight Simulator; therefore, their use must be done at your own risk:

- **Use mods at your own risk:** It may affect the stability and security of your Windows 10/11 device.
- **Mods aren't tested by Microsoft:** They don't own them nor operate them; the Microsoft Flight Simulator team is not responsible for any issues the mods will cause.
- **Possible incompatibility issues**: Future updates of Microsoft Flight Simulator may be incompatible with the installed mods. In order to avoid such issues, it is recommended to uninstall the mods prior to updating.
- **Achievements might not work**: Some functionalities might be unavailable while using mods.
- **Privacy concerns**: A mod creator may access your Xbox Live and device data; this is a potential risk to privacy.
- **Content rating:** Mods are not rated by ESRB or similar boards, and some content might not be suitable for players of all ages.

USING SDK FOR ADVANCED MODDING

Welcome to the Microsoft Flight Simulator Software Development Kit! This SDK allows you to create add-ons for Microsoft Flight Simulator, whether in the simulator's built-in toolset or developing with external tools.

Creating Add-Ons

Creating add-ons typically involves a combination of in-game tools, activated via Developer Mode, and external tools. In addition to the SDK, you'll also have other development tools, such as the 3D Studio Max glTF exporter plug-in, that help you integrate your add-ons with creative tools and interfaces.

Add-ons are developed as packages, which can typically be broken down into three major components:

1. Developer Mode

Enabling Developer Mode in Microsoft Flight Simulator allows access to multiple in-sim tools used to create scenery, add aircraft, design missions, and much more-all of which can be done in many cases without knowledge of programming or any other external tool.

2. Creative Assets

These are the models, sound effects, textures, and other elements that are required to make your own add-ons. The default assets available in Developer Mode will not be sufficient for most projects, and you will have to make your own.

3. Configuration Files

These files are packaged along with the creative assets and contain all the information that Microsoft Flight Simulator needs to incorporate your add-on into the game.

While you can create basic assets using Developer Mode's in-game tools, to fully exploit the system and create more complex and engaging add-ons, you'll want to bring all three components together. If you have experience programming or have built add-ons for previous versions of the simulator, there are also additional Programming APIs to help you get the most out of the SDK.

Creating quality add-ons for a simulation like Microsoft Flight Simulator can be complicated. We encourage you to start by reading the documentation, which is linked below:

SDK Contents: General overview of what's contained within the SDK.

SDK Overview and Using the SDK: Two pages filled with information about how to get set up.

Sample Files: Examples of file structures and usages

Release Notes: If new releases or changes are available.

Developers with experience in Microsoft Flight Simulator X or other simulation software should also consult the Frequently Asked Questions section of the Dev Support forum.

For a comprehensive overview of aircraft creation, see the How To Make An Aircraft tutorial.

For further reading, there's also a section with resources about handling some of the tricky parts of add-on development, although it is off-topic for the simulator-specific add-on development process.

If you are new to developing add-ons, we recommend developing simple in-game objects or scenery in Developer Mode before moving on to the complex ones such as aircraft or airports, or highly-detailed scenery.

We hope you have fun, and we cannot wait to see what you'll be creating for the Microsoft Flight Simulator Marketplace!

Note: For details about publishing to the Marketplace, click [here](#).

Using This Manual

This manual is a reference and not a read-through document. It is designed to allow you to look up information as you need it to complete your project. It contains a number of features to help you quickly find what you're looking for.

The Table Of Contents

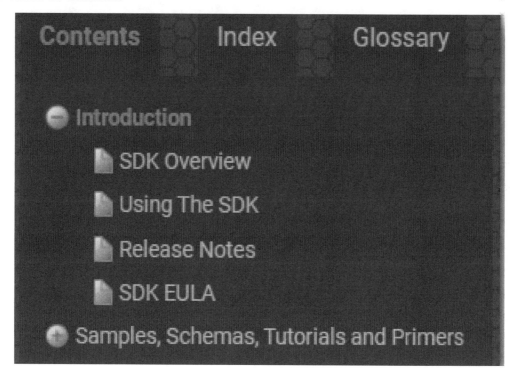

The Index

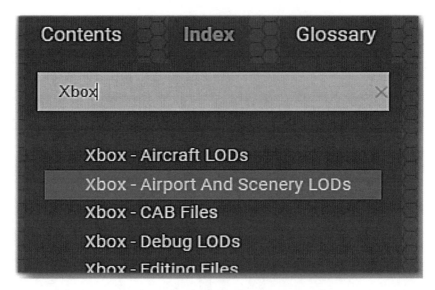

the glossary

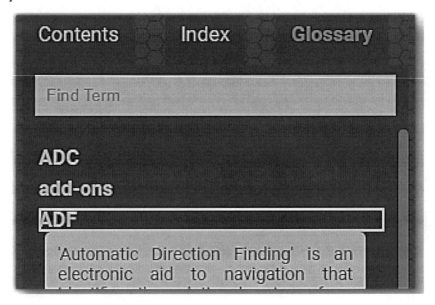

Search

The manual features a smart search system that not only shows pages containing the exact term you've entered but also pages that might not include that exact term but are still relevant to your search. To use the search, click the search button in the top right, enter your query, and press Enter to see the results in the search window.

Favorites

As there are so many pages covering various aspects, you may well find that some pages you refer to more frequently than others. In this case, you can easily "favorite" these. Just head to the page you want to save and click the favorite button to set it for quick access.

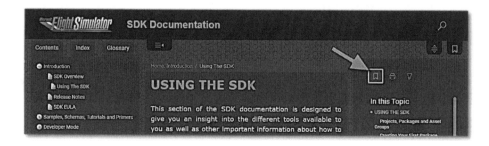

Once you have added a page to your favorites, you can view it by clicking on the favorites list button. This will show you all the pages you've marked as favorites.

You can edit your list by clicking the "pencil" icon and remove a page by clicking the "close" icon.

Additional Tools and Buttons

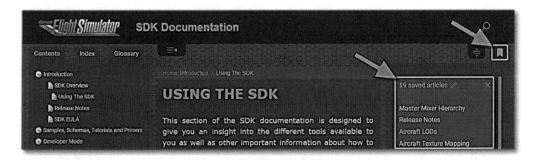

Hide ToC Button: This allows you to toggle the Table of Contents on the left side in and out of view.

Expand/Collapse Elements Button: Certain sections in the documentation, such as older Release Notes, are hidden under "spoilers." You can click this button to show or hide all spoilered sections in one go.

Print Page Button: Clicking this generates a printer-friendly version of the page and opens the browser's print dialogue.

Remove Highlights Button: After a search, keywords are highlighted on the page. Use this button to remove those highlights.

Back To Top Button: Scroll back to the top of the page in a second.

Fullscreen Button: Switch between going full screen and windowed. Fullscreen hides Table of Contents and page header and focuses on the main content.

Popular Third-Party Add-Ons

In Microsoft Flight Simulator 2024, any third-party content you download outside the simulator must be installed in your community folder, just like in MSFS 2020.

By default, the Community folder for MSFS 2024 is located in:

Steam:

C:\Users\[Your Username]\AppData\Roaming\Microsoft Flight Simulator 2024\Packages\Community

MS Store:

C:\Users\[Your Username]\AppData\Local\Packages\Microsoft.Limitless_8wekyb3d8bbwe\LocalCache\Packages\Community

It's important to make sure that any add-on mods you use are fully compatible with MSFS 2024. Using incompatible mods could cause issues with the simulator.

If you want to locate or change the Community folder:

1. Launch Microsoft Flight Simulator 2024

2. Open the Marketplace

3. Select "My Library"

4. Click "Settings" next to the search bar

5. Select "Open" to view the Community folder location

6. Select "Browse" to change the folder's location if desired

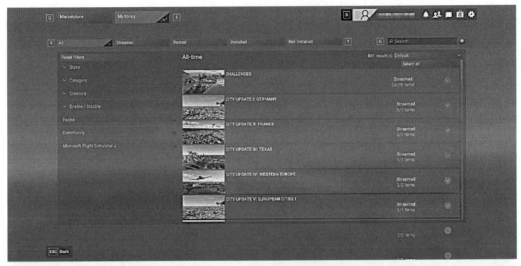

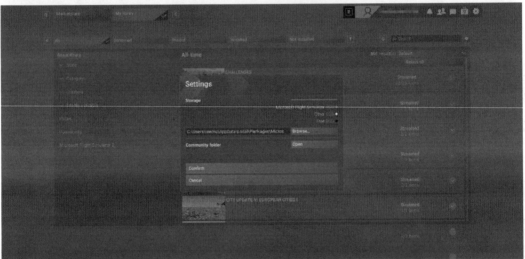

To verify that your add-ons are installed correctly, do the following:

1. Start Microsoft Flight Simulator 2024

2. Go to Marketplace

3. Click on "My Library"

4. Select "Community"

If your add-on(s) appear in this list, they are installed correctly.

INDEX

A

Add-ons and Mods for Enhanced Gameplay · 59
Advanced Avionics Setups · 24
Advanced Piloting Techniques · 91
Advantages of Training with a Flight Simulator · 81
Aircraft Approach Categories · 45
Aircraft Categories: From Props to Jets · 40
Aircraft Deep Dive · 66
Airport Override Checker Resolves Conflicts · 62
All Meanings of "Aircraft Category" · 44
All the parts of traditional Cessna 172 Cockpit · 70

B

Basics of Flight Simulation · 33
Best Gaming PC for Microsoft Flight Simulator 2024 · 31
Best Prebuilt PC for Microsoft Flight Simulator 2024 · 30
Bringing the World to Life · 124
Built-In Flight Lessons and Tutorials [Free] · 129

C

Certification Challenges and Achievements · 139
Challenges of Flight Simulator Training · 136
Choosing Flight Simulator Controls · 22
Commercial Airliners: Cockpits and Features · 68
community · 3, 4, 8, 19, 37, 39, 60, 62, 108, 111, 113, 120, 138, 155, 156, 158, 165
Customization and Modding · 158
Customizing Controls and Hotkeys · 56

D

DCS · 19, 21
Determining the Role of the Yoke in Aircraft Control · 72
Disadvantages of Flight Simulator Training · 82
Do Flight Simulators Enhance Flight Training? · 80

E

Emergency Procedures and Failures · 103

Enhancing Gameplay with Third-Party Tools · 155
Enhancing Skills with AI Assistance · 136
Expand Your View: Custom Camera Views for All Aircraft · 61
Exploring Global Destinations · 109
Exploring the Game Interface · 29

F

Famous Airports and Cities · 111
Final destinations · 51
Flying Conditions Made Real · 125
Frequently Asked Questions on VFR And IFR · 103

G

General Aviation Aircraft Overview · 67
Getting Started with MSFS 2024 · 11
Graphics and Performance Optimization · 52

H

Hidden Gems: Lesser-Known Locations · 115
Highlights of the New Features in MSFS 2024 · 8
How to choose the right VR headset · 141
How to Enable VR in Microsoft Flight Simulator · 32
How to Use Microsoft Flight Simulator 2024: · 77

I

Iconic Aircraft in MSFS 2024 · 75
IFR vs. VFR Flying · 97
Immersive Cockpit Experiences · 154
Inside a Real Flight Simulator Setup · 13

J

Joining the MSFS Community · 119

K

Key Techniques for Crosswind Takeoffs · 95

L

Lessons Learned: The Serious Flight Sim Enthusiast · 14

M

Mastering Takeoffs, Landings, and Crosswind Challenges · 93
Microsoft Flight Simulator 2024 · 1, 2, 3, 4, 5, 6, 7, 8, 9, 26, 27, 28, 29, 30, 31, 37, 38, 39, 46, 48, 49, 56, 59, 60, 61, 62, 63, 65, 77, 84, 88, 90, 93, 94, 103, 104, 105, 107, 108, 109, 110, 111, 112, 114, 115, 116, 118, 119, 120, 136, 137, 139, 143, 144, 145, 153, 165, 166, 167
Microsoft Flight Simulator 2024 Overview · 1

Minimum PC Requirements for MSFS2024 in VR · 152
Minimum System Requirements · 27
MSFS 2024 · 3, 7, 8, 9, 10, 11, 37, 38, 39, 40, 60, 65, 75, 77, 79, 112, 113, 114, 115, 120, 122, 137, 138, 143, 152, 153, 154, 165, 166
MSFS2024 In-Game Settings for Most GPUs · 151
MSFS2024. · 144, 154
Multiplayer and Community Features · 118

N

Navigating the World · 77
Nvidia Control Panel or Other GPU Interface · 156

O

Overview of the Guide and How to Use It · 4

P

Popular Third-Party Add-Ons · 165
Pros and Cons MSFS Flight Lessons · 130

R

Real-Time Multiplayer Flights · 122
Real-World Maps and Flight Paths · 79
Recommended System Requirements · 29

S

Safety Considerations at Airports with Obstacles · 96
Setting Up for Realism · 49
Setting Up VR for MSFS 2024 · 143
Staying Safe with VFR Flying · 100
Step-by-Step VR Optimization for GPUs · 145
Streamlining the Management of Add-Ons Using Addons Linker · 65
Suggestions to Improve the Experience of Engine Emergencies · 108
System Requirements and Installation · 26

T

The Importance of Emergency Training · 105
The Role of Weather and Navigation · 46
There are three major categories of lessons: · 131
Training and Learning Modules · 126
Types of Flight Simulators · 134

U

Understanding Aerodynamics in the Virtual World · 36
Understanding Crosswind Operations · 94
Unique Components of a Propeller Plane Cockpit · 74
Using Flight Simulators for Instrument Training · 83

Using SDK for Advanced Modding · 160
Using the World Map Interface · 84
Using Virtual Reality and Immersive Tools · 141

W

Welcome to Microsoft Flight Simulator 2024 · 2
What is an Aircraft Category? · 41
What You Need for a Flight Simulator · 12
What's the Best Flight Simulator for You? · 18
What's the Cost of a Home Flight Simulator? · 14
Which Monitor Should I Buy for Flight Simulators? · 23
Why Choose One-on-One Lessons? · 127
Why MSFS 2024 Is a Great VR Choice · 153
Why Pilots Choose IFR or VFR · 102